Salt Lake City

YESTERDAY & TODAY ™

Martha Sonntag Bradley and Elizabeth Bradley-Wilson

WEST
SIDE
PUBLISHING

This is the first writing collaboration between **Martha Sonntag Bradley** and her daughter **Elizabeth Bradley-Wilson.** Martha has an academic background in history and is an award-winning teacher at the College of Architecture and Planning at the University of Utah. She is also the dean of the school's Honors College. In 2008, she received the Honorary AIA Award from AIA Utah. Elizabeth makes historic preservation work a reality as assistant director of the Utah Heritage Foundation. She also manages the Revolving Loan Fund and Easement programs. Elizabeth, a talented poet and essayist, is the mother of two soccer stars, Aspen and Dylan, who are coached by their father and Elizabeth's husband, Mark Wilson.

Born and raised in Salt Lake City, photographer **Steve Greenwood** has chronicled the city's growth, beauty, and history against the magnificent backdrop of the Wasatch Mountains for more than 30 years. To view his photographic portfolio of Salt Lake City and Utah's many beautiful natural wonders, visit www.saltlakephotos.com.

Kirsten Hepburn is an accomplished fine art and commercial photographer. In capturing images for this book, she enjoyed exploring and documenting the many historic sites of Salt Lake City. You can see more of her work at www.hepburnphotography.com.

Mike Matson is a photographer and writer from Salt Lake City. He is the author of the guidebook *Moon Utah Camping,* and his photos have been published in the magazines *National Geographic Adventure, Backpacker, Northwest Travel,* and the *Utah Adventure Journal.* More of his work can be seen at www.mmatsonphoto.com.

Facts verified by **Hollie Deese.**

Salt Lake City stands before the majestic Wasatch Mountains in this photo from 2009.

CONTENTS

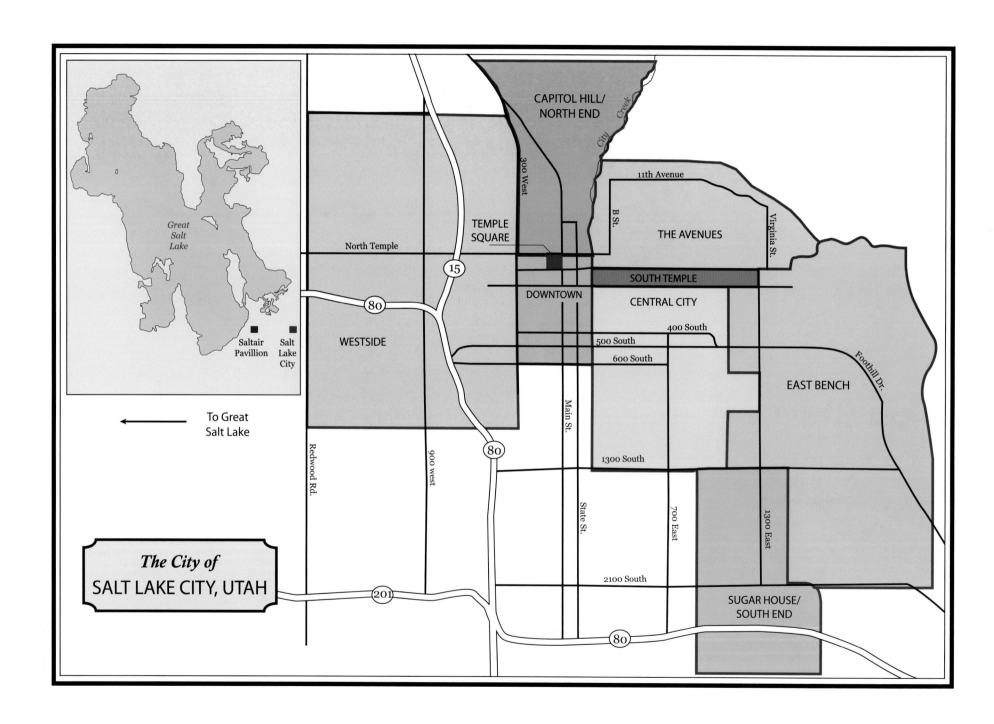

"THIS IS THE PLACE"

From its inception, Salt Lake City has been notably unique. While many other classic western towns such as Denver, Colorado, and Helena, Montana, slowly grew with the steady stream of fur trappers, miners, and farming families who drifted west, the valley that became Salt Lake City attracted the Mormons, a group sharing a single religious and moral vision. Cradled by the Great Salt Lake and the Wasatch and Oquirrh mountain ranges, the valley has distinct seasons: hot, dry summers; cold (but not severe) winters; and moderate springs. Here, cool creek waters flow down the foothills and lace through the valley floor.

Of course, the Mormons weren't the first to discover the region. Centuries before white settlers arrived, Native Americans traversed the valley—nomadic groups, including the Ute, Paiute, and Shoshone, all lived and hunted in the area. The Mormon pioneers who arrived in 1847 were members of a religious community that sought to build a new life after a failed similar effort in the Midwest. This time they succeeded: Salt Lake City became the headquarters of The Church of Jesus Christ of Latter-day Saints (LDS), the territorial capital, and a major regional supply station.

At the end of the first year, nearly 1,700 people lived in Salt Lake City; by 1850, that number had grown to approximately 6,157 people. The original plat extended three blocks to the east of Temple Square, nine blocks to the south, and five blocks to the west and north. By the time the railroad came to the city in 1870, more than 12,000 people lived in Salt Lake City. The population continued to rise between 1850 and 1890—the decade of Utah's statehood.

PROGRESSION AND THE PROGRESSIVE ERA

During the late 19th century and into the 1920s, an impulse for reform took storm in America, one that would shape the future of many U.S. cities and citizens. The Progressive Movement was born out of the hope for a return to the original Democratic ideals, particularly through widespread social, economic, and political reform. In 1910, a group of philanthropic society women in Salt Lake City organized the Children Aid Society to help orphans and poor children. Another group, known as the Free Kindergarten Association, founded the city's Neighborhood House in 1894, one of the country's first settlement houses. Yet another Progressive Era proposition, the City Beautiful movement, inspired the planting of trees in Washington

The quintessential symbol of the settlement of the American frontier, log cabins were built during the advance wave of community building in the Salt Lake Valley. This undated photo shows the oldest house in Salt Lake City, built in 1847.

Square and Liberty and Pioneer parks. An elaborately planted median down the middle of 1200 East and other streets created the equivalent of a boulevard found in larger cities. New playgrounds and parks expressed the Progressive Movement's "Muscular Christianity" ideal, particularly the notion that healthy kids made for robust and responsible citizens.

The beginning of the 20th century was a time of many changes for the city, some of them difficult. After seven unsuccessful attempts at statehood, Utah finally was accepted into the Union in 1896. But in gaining statehood, the LDS church had to enact the Manifesto of 1890, conceding and officially ending sanctioned polygamy (or plural marriage) for its members— an unpopular decision. Just a few years before statehood, like many cities throughout the nation, Salt Lake City suffered during the Panic of 1893 national economic depression. Markets for manufactured, mined, and agricultural products plummeted; it is estimated that 48 percent

of the city's workers were unemployed by the first months of 1894. Despite the strains caused by the depression, money from mining and railroad entrepreneurs helped Salt Lake City achieve economic prosperity again by the end of the 19th century.

In 1906, a civic improvement league formed in line with the national Progressive Movement's efforts to improve urban environments. The league pushed for infrastructure improvements in the city's sewer system and governmental systems. The city council approved the expansion of sidewalks beyond the downtown core to 1300 East and 900 South. The city was noticeably stretching outward.

WAXING AND WANING

Throughout the era, the city grew by dividing existing lots, and also by annexing farmland that connected to the city as the streetcar system expanded. First platted during the 1850s, nine new subdivisions made the Avenues a popular residential neighborhood, known for its close proximity to the city. Streetcar lines ran up both First and Third Avenues. Federal Heights, Gilmer Park, and the Ivy League streets just west of the university exhibited the city's increasing wealth and stratification. By 1910, the Sugar House district assumed its own identity as an incorporated town.

In the same way that the Progressive Era response prompted urban infrastructure projects, the New Deal's legacy was Works Progress Administration (WPA) projects such as new roads and road repairs, sewers, and guttering. The Civilian Conservation Corps, or CCC, built rock walls that framed the University of Utah campus and Reservoir Park. Responding to the deep and enduring impact of the 1929 Great Depression, the federal government made an impression on the city's landscape in numerous ways. By the time WPA was suspended in 1943, money had been poured into various new buildings and structures, both on campus and off.

During World War II numerous defense industries moved into the area because of the valley's transportation system, the city's location at the base of the Wasatch Mountains, and its ready supply of water. In the wake of the war, Salt Lake City adjusted to a new set of realities: suburbia and urban sprawl. Between 1950 and 1960, the city's population grew only 4 percent as families migrated to the suburbs. Fewer shoppers walked the city streets, and many businesses fell into disrepair. Fom the '60s through the '80s, Salt Lake City lost population. Bus ridership declined, and the city became dependent on the automobile. At mid-century, tourism became an important revenue source for the city. Temple Square itself attracted up to six million visitors each year. When the First Security Building was erected in 1955, it was the first new structure built downtown in approximately 31 years.

Located strategically on Main Street, the Walgreen Drugs soda counter was a favored hangout for shoppers or teenagers who wanted to dangle their feet for a while. The busy corner is shown here in 1940.

During the 2002 Winter Olympics, city buildings were draped with banners portraying athletes.

A GREAT PLACE TO LIVE AND WORK

According to the 2000 census, Salt Lake City has more than 181,000 residents. It's a youthful city with an average age of 30. The population continues to rebound since the drop in the '60s. Since 1995, the number of residential units in the central business district has practically doubled. New condominium and apartment projects along light rail lines and at Trolley Square, The Gateway, and Library Square have added hundreds of alternatives to the single-family detached home in neighborhoods close to urban amenities. By 2012, the planned City Creek development replacing the Crossroads and ZCMI malls will add new residential units downtown.

Salt Lake City has appeared on many top ten lists over the years. The Web site CNNMoney.com included the city as one of the 100 best places to live and launch businesses in 2008 because of its diverse population, ready access to 11 world-class ski resorts, and other entertainment amenities. Distinguished by a unique history, to be sure, Salt Lake City looks forward to the future.

KEY TO THE CITY

From the beginning, Salt Lake City was a sacred city for the Latter-day Saints, a belief rooted in a religious sense of a chosen people. Nineteenth-century Mormonism was an all-encompassing religious lifestyle distinguished by Sunday worship services but also by distinctive religious doctrines such as cooperation and polygamy. Religion shaped decisions about the placement of streets and houses, community institutions, and the way the city embraced the landscape. Although it is not in the actual center of the valley, Temple Square became a focal point, and all streets stretched north and south, east and west from there. Temple Square is the headquarters of The Church of Jesus Christ of Latter-day Saints.

The block immediately to the east of Temple Square is also the key to understanding the unique history of the city. The Bishop's Storehouse anchored the southeast corner; there the tithing yards and outbuildings to the side stored goods donated to the church by faithful members ready for distribution to the area's poor. To the south of the block, the Lion and Beehive houses and the church president's office lined the South Temple streetscape. Brigham Young's family homestead included a schoolhouse for his many children, orchards and gardens, beehives, and a two-story outhouse. By the end of the 19th century, the block also included three college buildings on the northwest corner and the houses of some of the plural wives of Young and Heber C. Kimball, his counselor in the First Presidency of the Latter-day Saint

church. If an urban space can tell a story, this single block completes the narrative of the LDS pioneer settlement of the Salt Lake Valley.

MOVEMENT ON MAIN STREET

Since the 1850s, Main Street has been the historic centerpiece of downtown Salt Lake City. Through the late 19th century, Main Street was lined with many different kinds of commercial buildings and establishments. By 1860 there were already 560 businesses in Salt Lake City, concentrated in the blocks surrounding the central area offering a range of services, including retail, dining, and manufacturing.

The city was compact, walkable, and commercial buildings were mixed with residences. In 1872, the city's first public

When this photo was taken in the early 1900s, Main Street was cluttered with electrical wires that were strung above the streets, and traffic that included horse-drawn wagons.

Left: The Salt Lake Temple stands tall on a lovely spring day in 2009.

and agricultural markets. Salt Lake City had arrived as a thriving western metropolis.

During the latter part of the 19th century and the early 20th century, a tense competition between Mormon and non-Mormon businessmen played out on Main Street. The division was not only by religion, but also by area: The non-Mormon Exchange Place and Odd Fellows Hall were situated farther south on Main Street while the LDS core was at the top of the north end, culminating with the Zions Cooperative Mercantile Institution (ZCMI), Hotel Utah, and the church headquarters.

STREETCAR SPRAWL

During the last few decades of the 19th century, streetcars connected the two ends of Main Street as well as streets to the east and west. The Rapid Transit Company laid tracks along State Street, First Avenue, 200 South, and lines to attractions such as White Sulphur Springs, Calder's Park, West Side Race Track, Smoot's Pleasure Gardens, and Beck's Hot Springs. These rail lines changed the residential pattern of the city, as workers were able to travel some distance from their homes to their jobs.

The growth pattern after the turn of the century was toward the edges of the city. In the 1950s and '60s, like most American cities, suburbanization characterized Salt Lake City, and many downtown businesses fled to the outskirts. The move depleted the energy and vitality of Main Street businesses and the urban core. Unfortunately, the construction of

On Statehood Day in 1896, ZCMI was bedecked with flags. Local papers announced, "UTAH IS A STATE AT LAST." The papers reported that a 128-foot by 150-foot American flag hung from the ceiling of the Tabernacle.

transportation—trolley cars towed by mules and horses—carried people and goods along South Temple and Main Street. The Salt Lake Railroad Company electrified its system in 1889. The upgrade left many bystanders in awe. According to one account, "The car sped up grades in fine style, and people along the line stared as though an apparition were flying by." By 1890, eight cars on nine miles of track connected workers and customers to businesses downtown.

With the increase in transportation, Salt Lake City saw a burst of growth at the turn of the century. As the city's population

grew, so did its business district. New manufacturing businesses moved toward the west part of town, to the industrial area surrounding the railroad depots. Mirroring the thriving mining and agricultural industries, the financial and professional areas of the city flourished as well. Tall steel-frame structures were erected, such as the Boston and Newhouse buildings, modeled after architect Louis Sullivan's work and the Chicago style of architecture. This obvious change to the local landscape marked the city's growing sophistication, as well as its dependence on national markets and wealth related to mining the Crossroads and ZCMI malls downtown in the '70s did little to reverse this trend.

GOVERNED BY THE PEOPLE, FOR THE PEOPLE

The separation of church and state in Salt Lake City hasn't always been black and white. For years, the LDS Church was considered the authority on all matters, and the line between church and state often blurred: During the 19th century, ceremonies that Mormons would later perform in the temple played out in the secular spaces of the Council Hall's upper level. When the civic power shifted from the church to the U.S. government in the 1850s, the city became the administrative center of state, county, and local government as well. Since then the territorial and state legislatures have met in Salt Lake City.

The Utah State Capitol is the heart of state governmental activities. A dramatic focal point of the city from virtually any point in the valley, the capitol's importance and prominence is emphasized by State Street, which literally ascends to the front steps of the capitol from a point on the opposite side of the valley.

Further down State Street, the City and County Building (built in the 1890s) and the Scott Matheson Courthouse (2000s) face each other on opposite sides of the street. Metaphorically, these buildings represent the important conversation and participation between the judicial and executive branches of government.

DOWNTOWN CULTURE

Within a decade of the first settlement in the 1840s, the townspeople were ready to create a cultured city as well as one dedicated to God. Sophisticated buildings were erected, modeled after East Coast and European examples. These buildings extended beyond the temple site to include the Social Hall (1852), Salt Lake Theater (1862), and Council Hall (1866). Eventually, the blocks bordering Young's home also featured the LDS Business College, mansions, and a theater.

For generations, the Salt Lake Theater and the Social Hall provided backdrops for theatricals, dances, banquets, musicals, and just about every other type of social event imaginable. During Brigham Young's lifetime, the theater, designed by church architect William Folsom, was one of the most significant pieces of architecture in the valley. A great lover of theater, Young advocated a balanced life of righteous living to be sure, but one filled with culture, art, and music.

Today, Salt Lake City continues to make culture and entertainment a priority. The Bicentennial Arts Complex located on West Temple includes the Abravanel Symphony Hall and the Salt Lake Art Center. The Salt Lake Art Center's contemporary exhibits feature both local and national artists and offers classes as well. The Capitol Theatre, located just around the corner on 200 South between Main Street and West Temple, is the home to the Utah Opera and Ballet West.

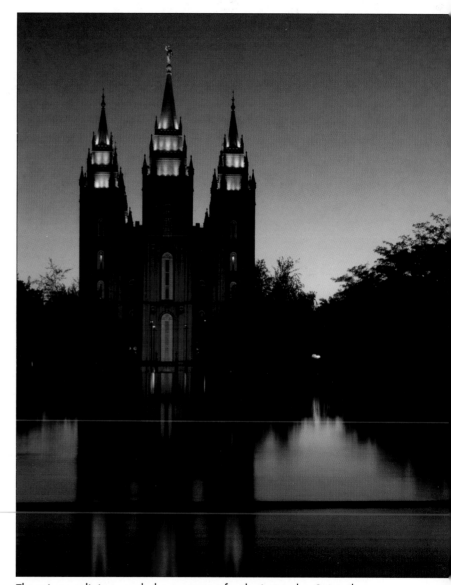

There is no religious symbol more potent for the Latter-day Saints than the Salt Lake Temple. Mormons consider temple worship the high point of their religious lives.

This view of the LDS Conference Center in 2009 makes reference to Meso-American temples of Central America, the landscape of narratives from the Book of Mormon, and Latter-day Saint scripture.

LDS CONFERENCE CENTER

In the mid-19th century, the Church of Jesus Christ of Latter-day Saints built three structures on Temple Square for general church conferences: a bowery (1847), the Old Tabernacle (1852), and the historic Tabernacle (1864), each with an increased capacity for seating. But it would be the beginning of the 21st century before they would build an entirely new auditorium—the LDS Conference Center.

Unarguably, the LDS Conference Center is massive—the building fills up most of a ten-acre city block. In fact, it is believed to be the world's largest auditorium built for worship. As many as 21,000 churchgoers can sit comfortably in the main auditorium to listen to General Authorities at the church's biannual General Conference and other church events. A smaller Conference Center Theater is used for various theatrical, musical, and other cultural events throughout the year. The roof is terraced to the east with plants native to Utah's mountainous landscapes, where visitors can stroll through the lush gardens and gaze into a reflective pond. It is easy to orient oneself to the rest of the LDS Church headquarters campus by the steeple that establishes the building as a religious structure.

Creating such a large auditorium (seen here in recent times) was no easy task. It took three construction companies working in tandem to handle the scope of this building project—on any given day as many as 1,000 workers were on-site.

General Conferences held in both April and October bring members of the Church of Jesus Christ to Salt Lake City, where they receive instruction from the General Authorities of the Church. In 1942, members could record their attendance on this board, which hung on the wall surrounding Temple Square.

One of the city's most important architectural projects during the 19th century was the Salt Lake Temple. Brigham Young appointed his brother-in-law Truman O. Angell Sr. to design and manage the temple construction. The city, with the temple in the middle, is seen here in 1912.

TEMPLE SQUARE

On April 6, 1893, cheers of "Hallelujah!" and thousands of white handkerchiefs filled the air as Latter-day Saints celebrated the completion of the Salt Lake Temple. In total, 75,000 people—far more than the population of Salt Lake City at the time—participated in the dedication ceremonies. The temple was finished after 40 years of construction delays and social disruption due to the Federal anti-polygamy crusades of the late 1800s.

Temple Square forms the heart of Salt Lake City. Distinguishable from other city blocks by its looming 15-foot-tall adobe walls, the sacred space includes the Salt Lake Temple, the Salt Lake Tabernacle, the Assembly Hall, and the Visitor's Center. As a landmark, the temple represents the sacrifice of the Mormon pioneers, their industry, and their devotion to God. The building's six towers and spires and the iconic gold-leaf statue of the Angel Moroni form the distinctive signature of the Salt Lake Temple as well as the city's skyline.

Workers stop for a photo op in 1879. Brigham Young was active in dictating the design of the Salt Lake Temple. In spring 1853, he visited Angell's office and sketched the temple he had in mind, complete with six towers.

Workers in 1952 spruce up the statue of Moroni. Paris-trained Utah sculptor Cyrus Dallin created the first Angel Moroni to appear on the top spire of an LDS temple. Moroni, a Book of Mormon figure, represents a messenger heralding the restoration of the ancient religion for a new dispensation, as was foretold in Mormon scripture.

In this photo from 1872, stonemasons quarry quartz monzonite (granite) for the Salt Lake Temple at Little Cottonwood Canyon, 20 miles from the center of town. The stones were then hauled by oxen and mules to the construction site.

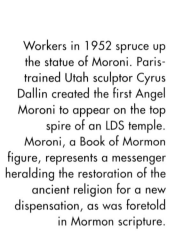

In the temple ritual, the Celestial Room is the pinnacle, the symbolic representation of the worshipper's having arrived at the presence of God. The Celestial Room is not necessarily a meeting room, but an in-between space. It is considered particularly special by Mormons and is entered only by those who have completed the temple ritual itself. The room is seen here in 1911.

THE SALT LAKE TABERNACLE

Casting its own unusual silhouette in the skyline, the oval-shape Salt Lake Tabernacle has a silver elliptical roof, resembling a great inverted bowl perched upon 44 red sandstone buttresses. The tabernacle was built from 1864 to 1867 by Henry Grow and later, Truman O. Angell Sr. Workers used leftover materials from the temple and tabernacle projects to construct the Assembly Hall located in the southwest corner of the square.

773   TABERNACLE ORGAN AND CHOIR, GREAT MORMON TABERNACLE, SALT LAKE CITY, UTAH

64621

Bottom left: Distinguished for its distinctive shape as well as its unusual construction methodology—no nails were used to build the massive truss system—the Salt Lake Tabernacle also houses an elaborate 11,623-pipe organ. In this undated photo, a man stands amid the inner workings of the pipes. *Above:* This 1916 postcard shows another local highlight: concerts by the world-famous Tabernacle Choir.

A favorite Christmas activity during the weeks between Thanksgiving and New Years is visiting Temple Square to see the Christmas lights, as seen here in 2008. A virtual winter wonderland, the LDS church strings thousands of strands of colorful lights on virtually every upright structure from trees to wrought iron fences. Floating candles in the reflecting pool at Main Street Plaza complete the effect.

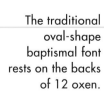

The traditional oval-shape baptismal font rests on the backs of 12 oxen.

BRIGHAM YOUNG

LDS CHURCH PRESIDENT, prophet, governor, husband, father—Brigham Young made an impact that was colorful, dramatic, and intentional. Young masterminded the settlement of a vast region—the Great Basin Kingdom—and directed the establishment of more than 400 towns along the basic guidelines of the Plat of the City of Zion, handed down to the Latter-day Saints from their first church president, Joseph Smith.

Utah Territory provided a refuge to the Mormon Saints who fled there after conflicts with non-Mormons in the Midwest. It was left to Young to organize their exodus first out of Nauvoo, Illinois, and then Winter Quarters, Nebraska. Young placed church members in teams led by captains and composed stratified communities. He organized the colonization of the territory in much the same way, building settlement teams who would travel to a new unexplored area, draw up a plat map, distribute property, and work together to build irrigation systems and meetinghouses. In a tangible way, these "Saints," or followers of Jesus Christ, demonstrated their faith and commitment to a particular religious way of life modeled and in some ways conceptualized by Young himself.

Young is also known for his dozens of wives (and more than 50 children). His own family complex on the block immediately east of Temple Square included two large homes designed to accommodate the complex lifestyle of a polygamous family: a schoolhouse, orchard, vegetable garden, and outbuildings. All the components of the good life—religion, education, and hard work—that Young sought for the rest of the church started at his own homestead.

MAIN STREET PLAZA

Main Street Plaza is a shaded, beautifully landscaped respite from the busy city center. The historic wall surrounding Temple Square opens up to the plaza, creating convenient access to the flower and sculpture gardens to the west. The plaza's centerpiece is a large circular reflecting pool that often mirrors the Salt Lake Temple towering above.

Throughout the 20th century, this same serene street was the scene of occasional protests against the LDS church. Demonstrators who supported the Equal Rights Amendment in the 1970s, for instance (and who opposed the church's campaign against the ERA), shouted through megaphones to disrupt the LDS General Conferences being held in the Tabernacle at Temple Square, or interfered with wedding parties posing on the steps of the temple. In a deal negotiated by former Mayor Deedee Corradini and LDS leaders, the block of public land was sold to the church in 2001.

A debate surrounding the land deal followed, but it was agreed that the need for continuous pedestrian traffic through downtown was critical. As a result, in 2002 previous pedestrian restrictions were eased—restrictions that had regulated use of the plaza by demonstrators, persons with "ghetto blasters," or "unmodest" clothing—basically, the sort of realism and diversity found in most major American cities.

But the church had its own vision: Main Street Plaza had not been conceptualized as a vital urban space, but as a connecting thread in the LDS church headquarters campus. The plaza offered an enhanced connection between the area's various buildings: the LDS Church Office Building, the Beehive and Lion houses, the Joseph Smith Memorial Building, and the cluster of sacred structures at Temple Square. In a way, the plaza and the two LDS-centric blocks surrounding it narrate a story about the life of a Latter-day Saint, the church's history, and its relationship with the city as a whole.

Pictured above is Main Street Plaza, as seen in the late 1800s (top) and 1947 (bottom). For years, people debated over the proper location for the landmark Brigham Young statue before it was put in its current space at the intersection between Main Street and North Temple.

Holiday lights
illuminate Main Street
Plaza.

LDS CHURCH OFFICE BUILDING

Standing 28 stories tall, the modernist LDS Church Office Building was erected between 1962 and 1972 and was inspired by Le Corbusier and the International Style of Architecture. Housing the General Authorities support staff and the administrative team for the LDS church and its various auxiliary organizations, the building is found on the northeast edge of the church's downtown Salt Lake City campus and at the end of the plaza.

Welcoming visitors to the building is a massive mural in the central lobby painted by Seventh-day Adventist artist Harry Anderson, depicting Jesus Christ instructing the Apostles to preach for him throughout the world. On it is the inscription, "That the struggles, sacrifices and the sufferings of the faithful pioneers and the cause they represented shall never be forgotten." On the building's exterior are panels with the earth's two hemispheres, representing the church's continuous worldwide missionary efforts.

Above left: The LDS Administration Building was built in 1917 and is seen here at mid-20th century. It is reserved for the offices of the General Authorities of the Church of Jesus Christ of Latter-day Saints: the First Presidency (the church president and his two counselors), the Twelve Apostles, and the offices of the Seventies. *Above right:* In front of the tall Church Office is a statue of Brigham Young with one of his wives, Emma Smith.

Pictured above is a 19th-century view of the Beehive House (on the left) and Eagle Gate.

BEEHIVE HOUSE AND THE LION HOUSE

As territorial governor and president of the Church of Jesus Christ of Latter-day Saints, Brigham Young welcomed visitors to the Salt Lake Valley at the Beehive House. Young and several of his wives and children lived in the two historic houses designed by temple architect Truman Angell Sr. in 1847—the Beehive House and the Lion House.

After arriving in the Salt Lake Valley in a series of wagon trains in 1847, many of Young's wives were housed first in a pioneer fort before moving into log buildings on "log row" in 1848. Six years after their arrival in the valley, construction started on the Beehive House, built as Young's official and public residence, which he shared with one of his wives, Lucy Ann Decker, and their seven children. He built the governor's office next door, as well as the Lion House, bookending his office.

Inside the Beehive House, its namesake, a beehive, was carved into the cupola, symbolizing the economy and industry characteristic of the pioneer generation. Young added a two-story porch across the full length of the facade in 1869, adding dignity to the plaster-covered adobe building. His first-floor office was plain and only about 25 square feet. Young's large writing desk, money safe, various tables, chairs, sofas, and a fancy store-bought rug gave the impression that the president of the LDS church was a person of some means and sophistication.

In 1959, the Beehive House was restored and opened for visitors.

BRINGING WORK HOME WITH YOU

The blending of Beehive House and the Church President's Office (seen in this photo to the far right and left, respectively)—the two buildings share contiguous walls and an architectural style—suggest the complexity of Brigham Young's role in Utah Territory. At various times church president, territorial governor, colonizer, and negotiator, Young's unusual lifestyle invited public commentary. Unarguably, he was a mover and shaker whose vision for the good life at the foothills of the Wasatch Mountains brought Mormonism into a new era.

Bottom left: The Beehive House Museum retains the home's original opulence. *Bottom right:* One can find the beehive symbol throughout the home. When Utah Territory petitioned the federal government in 1849 as the State of Deseret for permission to join the Union, it evoked the symbol of the beehive. *Deseret* is a Book of Mormon word for "honeybee." Since that time, the beehive symbol is a sentimental favorite of the region.

THE LION HOUSE

The Lion House is one of the most unique pieces of architecture in the Great Basin region, demonstrating in physical form the complexities of life in a plural family. Wives in their childbearing years were given choice rooms on the upper floor, giving them access to their children as well as their shared husband. Elegant in ways befitting the home of the territorial and religious leader, the Lion House was both provincial and cosmopolitan at the same time.

LIFE IN THE YOUNG HOUSEHOLD

As a polygamist, Brigham Young had many mouths to feed. Although Mormon records state that at the time of his death in 1877, Young had married as many as 56 women, he apparently didn't regard them all as "wives" in the traditional sense. Instead, many were widows or elderly women under his care. As early as 1859, he was reported to have 15 wives and 57 children (46 of whom survived to adulthood). The Young homestead took up much of the block, including multiple houses, a two-story outhouse, beehives, gardens, an orchard, and a schoolhouse where his children studied. His family grew enough food on-site to be self-sufficient.

To say that family life within the Lion House was complex would be an understatement: As many as 12 of his wives, 19 daughters, and 8 sons shared the family home and its 20 bedrooms. The Lion House also reflects many of Young's conceptions regarding physical health: Closed-in porches gave children the chance to breathe clean air during the nighttime, gymnasium equipment was provided for the children, and generous connecting spaces enabled the children to move freely through the home and into the yard beyond.

JOSEPH SMITH MEMORIAL BUILDING/ FORMER HOTEL UTAH BUILDING

In 1909, the LDS church tore down the longtime favorite Salt Lake City landmark, the Bishop's Storehouse—the center of the church's tithing industries—to build the Hotel Utah. Opened in 1911, the new hotel served as a place to meet visiting dignitaries or people doing business with Mormon-owned operations. Non-Mormons were among the hotel's stockholders, but this extravagant hotel primarily represented the church's effort to reach beyond the borders of the state to national markets.

When discussion began over the Hotel Utah's future in the 1990s, an extensive economic analysis determined it was no longer viable as a hotel. Debate over whether it should be torn down to make way for a more modern structure or receive an extensive restoration inspired local historic preservationists to lobby the LDS church to save the building. The church hired local firm FFKR Architects to design the adaptive reuse of the hotel as an office building that would enhance the church's mission and downtown presence.

The exterior was restored to its original appearance with little variation. A plaster-and-brick beehive cupola was returned to its previous location on the building's rooftop. The interior faced the most changes, including completely gutting the ten existing hotel floors and reconfiguring them to eight levels with open-plan office environments. New features included a 500-seat theater where films are shown that teach church history and its missionary message. Restaurants and reception rooms run along the building's top floor. In 1993, it reopened as the Joseph Smith Memorial Building.

The Joseph Smith Memorial Building is shown here in 2009. Inside, the restoration team returned the grand lobby and the main-floor Empire Room to their original beauty.

The top of the Hotel Utah caught fire on July 14, 1912, just one year after the hotel opened. Spectators watch the billowing smoke on Main Street looking north from 200 South.

The Hotel Utah (seen here in 1911) had 500 elegant rooms. Although controversial with Church President Joseph F. Smith, a first-floor bar was a required amenity for traveling businessmen from outside the area. A grand lobby, ballroom, and other meeting rooms made the hotel a favorite for staging events.

Utah architects FFKR led the rehabilitation of Hotel Utah that included transforming the building from a hotel into office space, an LDS chapel, and a downtown branch of the LDS bookstore. Although it was not historically in the lobby, a monumental statue of Joseph Smith establishes the religious purpose of the building that today combines the secular and spiritual functions of the church in a single public building.

The Zion's Cooperative Mercantile Institution's (ZCMI) first headquarters was built in 1869 in the Eagle Emporium building with other "departments" located along Main Street. In 1876, the ZCMI shops were consolidated in a single impressive store on Main Street. Architects Obed Taylor and William H. Folsom designed the original brick and cast-iron facade. A later addition in 1880 doubled the building's square footage. The ZCMI is shown here on November 2, 1910.

UPPER MAIN STREET

During the first decades after settlement, small family-run businesses were located along Main Street, the commercial core in a fledgling town. Shops had false fronts with simple single- or two-story adobe or wood buildings behind them, giving the appearance of a Hollywood frontier town. In 1850, James M. Livingstone and Charles A. Kinkead began the first store on Main Street—a small building on the corner of First North and West Temple. The Walker Brothers store (which initially was a dry goods shop but by 1871 included a bank) sat on one side of the street facing the Eagle Emporium at 102 South Main Street, the city's oldest commercial building (that now houses a Zion's Bank branch).

From the first, the density of commercial activity established the top of Main Street as the city's business center. After the railroad came to town in the 1870s, a growing diversity of goods, businesses, and persons flooded into town; Main Street functioned as a sort of supply station, providing dry goods, boarding rooms, and plenty of saloons, earning it the nickname "Whiskey Street." Granted, Main Street itself was nothing much—dusty during the summer months, and mucky and rutted from late fall to spring. Eventually improvements were made: wooden sidewalks along the storefronts and hitching posts where horses lazily waited for their owners to return.

In 1868, a group of Mormon businessmen met in the Council Hall. Their leader, Brigham Young, wanted to combat the growing power of non-Mormon businesses in town. Together, the men joined forces to create the Zion's Cooperative Mercantile Institution (ZCMI). Brought under the cooperative umbrella, their independent businesses functioned as America's first department store. Their plan was a success: Within a few years, ZCMI branch stores were found throughout the territory, and many non-Mormon stores were edged out of the competition.

Shoppers converge around the Walker Bank Building on Main Street and 200 South in September 1920. For years after it was built in 1912, the 20-story Walker Bank Building held the honor of being the tallest west of the Mississippi River. Described by *The Salt Lake Tribune* as "but another step typifying the new Salt Lake City, a metropolis which is destined to be unrivaled between Chicago and San Francisco," the building publicized the "strides this city is taking."

By the mid-20th century, trolleys had been removed from the streets and replaced by cars, buses, and other motorized transportation. This view of Main Street in 1949 shows the bustling commercial district, recovering from both the deprivation of the Great Depression and the war years. And nothing exhibits a more hopeful promise of better days ahead than a streetscape lined with elegant skyscrapers, storefronts, and restaurants open for business.

KEARNS BUILDING

On par with the finest new tall buildings built throughout the United States, the 1909–1911 Kearns building is a steel-frame building modeled after the Chicago–style structures by Louis Sullivan. Thomas Kearns was the quintessential self-made man. A poor miner when he first arrived in Salt Lake City, in less than a decade he was a silver-mining magnate, United States senator, and part owner of *The Salt Lake Tribune*. Both the Kearns and the Walker Bank buildings are in use today, filled with law offices and a wide range of commercial activities.

During the 2002 Winter Olympics, area buildings such as the One Utah Center designed by Niels Valentiner became the equivalent of a stage set. Colossal murals of Olympic athletes were hung from rooftops to ready the city for the international celebration.

The Promised Valley Playhouse is shown in the late 1950s (left) and today (below). Since its initial opening in 1905 as the Orpheum Theatre, a wide variety of vaudeville acts have passed through, including Nellie Florede, described by *The Salt Lake Tribune* as "winsome, pretty and chic," and the Three Jacksons, a group that performed a "scientific boxing bout and engaged in other athletic exercises that stamped them as artists in their class."

PROMISED VALLEY PLAYHOUSE/ FIRST ORPHEUM THEATRE

On a chilly Christmas Day in 1905, the Orpheum Theatre opened to a packed house. Located near the historic site of the Salt Lake Theatre, the Orpheum's facade featured a 12-foot-tall statue of the goddess Venus and two large stone busts of Zeus. The crowd was eager to see the scheduled vaudeville performance. Over the years, virtually every type of vaudeville, from comedy skits to boxing matches and burlesque dancers performed on the Orpheum stage.

Eventually the theater was converted into a motion picture studio. It was renamed several times, including the Wilkes, the Roxey, and the Lyric. In the 1970s, the LDS church bought the building and staged performances of the *Promised Valley* musical there, renaming the theater the "Promised Valley Playhouse." In 1996, the theater was closed due to structural problems. In 2002, the majority of the building was torn down. But the three-story building was reborn once more as office space, complete with contrasting stone trim. The theater's old facade was reattached to the modern office building and parking terrace in what is sometimes called a "facadectomy."

When a concert or festival lights up the Gallivan Center at night (seen here in 2009), it epitomizes what defines a successful public space—a place where life, energy, and goodwill prevail, connecting people throughout the city.

GALLIVAN CENTER

More than perhaps any other space in Salt Lake City, the John W. Gallivan Utah Center demonstrates the importance a truly public place holds within a city. In fact, the center hosts a range of events that mirror the city's diversity, including Thursday night summer and "Lunch Bunch" concerts and "Opera in the Park" nights. Opened in 1993, the center features an amphitheater, an ice rink that converts to a pond in the summer, and public art. The Gallivan Center actually is the focal point between four major buildings that anchor the block: the One Utah Center,

Wells Fargo Center, Brooks Arcade, and the Marriott City Center, all framing a vibrant, lively public space on the interior. As a place for the people, it is regularly the stage for festivals, debates, poetry readings, parades, and exhibits.

Art is important to the center's exterior and interior. At the entrance on Main Street is *Peace Cradle,* a bronze sculpture of two kneeling children playing cat's cradle by Utah County artist Dennis Smith. *Story Wall* by Day Christensen borders the plaza's sunken lawn

area, featuring 82 bronze panels depicting Native American legends drawn by children.

The most prominent piece of art at the Gallivan is *Asteroid Landed Softly* by architecture professor Kazuo Matsubayashi, a towering sundial made of pink and sandstone boulders supported on twin columns clad in copper and reflective glass. According to Matsubayashi, the intent of the piece was to remind the plaza's visitors to slow down and "observe and interact with our environment."

At First Night, the citywide celebration of New Year's Eve, the Gallivan Center lights up with concerts, food booths, and street artists. Bundled up against the cold, families are entertained until the ringing in of the new year at midnight.

The One Utah Center, Salt Lake City's best-known postmodern building, references the historic materiality of downtown buildings with granite wall panels and colors that mirror the earth tones of the surrounding mountain range.

A sundial that interacts with the changing seasons, the design for *Asteroid Landed Softly* by Kazuo Matsubayashi was the result of a design competition that asked artists to create public art that responded to the valley's natural landscape.

Work continues on the city's new public library in January 2003, a dramatic addition to its downtown area. Construction crews carved out an urban open space defined by an amphitheater, walking paths, sitting areas, and public art.

SALT LAKE PUBLIC LIBRARY

Perhaps no other building has shaken up the city as much as the Salt Lake Public Library. Opened in February 2003, the building is a striking crescent, challenging the strict regularity of the city's streets and parallel orientation of the majority of downtown buildings. The new library engages both 200 East and 400 South in different and exciting ways: From the west, the building seems to be a rectangle with regularly placed windows and an entrance at the corner of the intersection. But viewed from the north, the building appears to be a sweeping sliver of glass.

From the southeast, the building moves naturally from its plaza to an amphitheater used during summer months for outdoor concerts and festivals. Visitors can walk along the six-story crescent wall to a rooftop garden, or simply take the elevator.

Inside, the new library is double in size from its predecessor, holding more than 500,000 books and materials, with ample room for more.

The most dramatic interior space is the glass-enclosed Urban Room, a vestibule complete with shops, bistros, and tables for library patrons to sit, chat, and enjoy the view of the mountains in the distance. The library was built with an $84 million bond from the city as part of the dramatic reshaping of the majority of the block. The library board selected Canadian-Israeli Moshe Safdie and Associates to design the building. "The library is not just a place for research and study, but it is a major meeting place that draws citizens from all across the city. It was something that really excited me," Safdie said. "It seemed that the program was sort of tailored to us."

During the Utah Arts Festival (shown here in 2008) held every summer in the last week of June, the outdoor space of Library Square is transformed into a village of sorts packed with vendor booths, food stands, and plenty of entertainment.

Above: Although it would be difficult to choose one space over another at the Salt Lake Public Library as being the best, the Urban Room would be a strong contender with its beautiful views, shops, and cafés. *Right:* It is easy to see how the Project Bandaloop dancers were inspired in their art by rock climbing, an indigenous mountain sport in the Salt Lake canyons. Performing in 2005 for the Utah Arts Festival, this aerial dance troupe engaged the vertical space along the library itself in the best tradition of public art—by activating public space.

HISTORIC SALT LAKE CITY PUBLIC LIBRARY

In the fall of 1850, the territorial legislature solicited federal aid to establish a regional library with William C. Staines serving as librarian. Along with children's aid and air pollution, public lending libraries became the focus of the Masonic Orders and the Ladies Literary Club of Salt Lake City, both of whom sponsored the 1898 bill that provided a tax levy in support of public libraries. With the help of mining magnate John Q. Packard, the Ladies Literary Club successfully campaigned for a separate library building at 15 South State Street, which opened in 1905.

The New York architectural firm Heins and La Farge designed the Salt Lake City Public Library building with the formal classical and Beaux Arts–style decorative elements often seen during this era.

By 1964, the library had clearly outgrown its location, and the collection was moved to the block across from the City and County Building. In 1968, an addition was built onto the building and until 2003, it was the home of the Hansen Planetarium. The building remained vacant until 2007, when local jewelers O. C. Tanner Co. bought the site to house its flagship store.

Top: The Salt Lake City Library stands on Main Street in 1905. Later, it would be used as the Hansen Planetarium. Upon entering the building, one would find two expansive stairways that led to the lecture hall on the second level. On the main floor was a sunny reading room with a librarian's desk in the center. *Bottom:* Men work at the study tables in the library's main reading room in 1917.

THE LEONARDO/FORMER SALT LAKE CITY MAIN LIBRARY

In the 1960s, the Salt Lake City Main Library was a state-of-the-art facility that represented the city's forward-thinking attitude. Almost as soon as it opened, the clean, modern-looking library won both national and local awards for its design excellence. Architectural firm Edwards & Daniels designed the building as an example of the new formalist style of architecture.

The Main Library was part of the city's plan to modernize, incorporating good transportation choices and new business, entertainment, recreational, and commercial opportunities downtown.

The library collection moved to its current location on the same block when the new building opened in 2003. In 2008, the library became the home of The Leonardo, a culture, science, and documentary arts center. For its first joint show, the center hosted the world-renowned Body Worlds 3 exhibit.

New formalist architecture, as seen in The Leonardo (formerly the Salt Lake City Main Library), features hanging panels behind which glass walls enclose an open space.

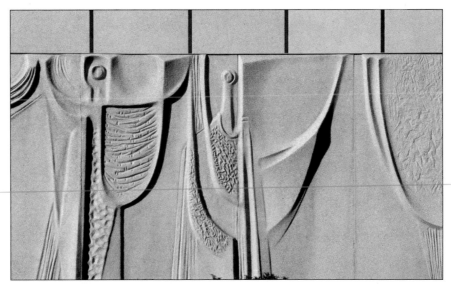

The bas relief panels on the building exterior are abstract, a modern version of the ancient bas relief sculptures that once adorned Gothic cathedrals.

Not long after the Salt Lake City and County Building was dedicated in early 1894, Congress passed the Utah Statehood Enabling Act. The building is shown here in 1902.

SALT LAKE CITY AND COUNTY BUILDING

There is a strong national propensity for using staid, classical styles for public buildings. The style of the Salt Lake City and County Building, however, is technically Richardson Romanesque. Viewed from above, the building's plan is in the shape of a Greek cross with four equal-size wings. Built with Kyune sandstone, a familiar material found in Utah, it is a building that in every way is rooted in this particular place and culture.

The building's exterior is awash in rich bas relief sculptural ornamentation, depicting the story of the city's history, leaders, and political issues. You will find busts of former mayors Jedediah M. Grant and Robert N. Baskin; women leaders such as Eliza R. Snow and Emmeline B. Wells, who participated in the national suffrage movement; traditional freemasonry symbols;

and the American eagle. Familiar images representing justice, industry, and sacrifice delineate the roofline, as well as sea monsters, gargoyles, suns, beehives, and other symbology.

Once the city decided to build the structure, conflict plagued the design and construction process from 1891 to 1894. Rivalry between the church-backed People's Party and the non-Mormon Liberal Party surfaced in a debate over whether the building was an unnecessary extravagance. During the years since its construction, the building has served multiple purposes, including the center of city, county, and territorial government; and for the parallel functions of city hall and the county court. Currently, city offices occupy the building, including the city council chambers.

Above: When it was announced in July 1995 that Salt Lake City had secured the 2002 Olympic Winter Games, more than 40,000 people celebrated outside the City and County Building. The five Olympic rings on the building stayed lit throughout the wintery Olympic nights.

The Salt Lake City and County Building's central clock tower rises 256 feet from the ground. In 1989, the city celebrated the end of a three-year, $31 million renovation of the historic building.

The interior continues the building's Richardsonian Romanesque style in its round arches, deep window recesses, and enormous columns. Beautiful multicolor onyx tile work enlivens the space.

SCOTT M. MATHESON COURT COMPLEX

Before 2000, the Third District Juvenile and District Courts met in the Metropolitan Hall of Justice. Forty years later, the Metropolitan was deemed unsafe and out of date, and it was readied for demolition to make way for the new Salt Lake Public Library. For years, the various functions of the courts were held in different locations. And so it was a matter of efficiency to bring the various courts, including the Utah State Supreme Court, under the same roof.

Embedded in the Scott M. Matheson Court Complex's design is the long tradition of public architecture and the classical style. The complex stands as an impressive landmark on State Street, only a few blocks south of the State Capitol and across the street from the Salt Lake City and County Building.

Top: The Scott M. Matheson Court Complex sits in the foreground in 2009. *Bottom:* Another side of the courthouse is shown in this photo from 2007. At the middle of the court complex, a large central rotunda faces the street. Because of the increase in contemporary security measures after the 1995 Oklahoma City federal building bombing, this entrance space plays a critical role in regulating who is allowed in the building and when.

EXCHANGE PLACE

The district created by mining entrepreneur Samuel Newhouse at the south end of Main Street's commercial district embodies the competition between Mormon and non-Mormon businessmen in the late 19th and early 20th centuries, a sort of tug-of-war that played out in architecture and public space. Newhouse hoped that Exchange Place would rival New York City's Wall Street, as a western commercial district built on mining wealth and riches gained from the expansion of the railroad. His initial design included 15 buildings—far more than would ever be built. Even so, the up-to-date, technologically contemporary buildings create one of the most intriguing interior spaces found on a Salt Lake City block. Each building has a steel frame, terracotta and masonry fireproofing, elevators, and the most advanced amenities available at the time, such as pneumatic tube systems.

During the late 19th century, Salt Lake City evolved from a theologically focused supply station to an important regional commercial center connected to national markets by the railroad. The city also fed off the immense wealth that poured out of Utah mines and into the pockets of wealthy mining entrepreneurs such as Newhouse, Thomas Kearns, and David Keith.

When this photo was taken in the 1960s, Exchange Place was still considered the most vital business district in Salt Lake City. In the foreground on the right is the Boston Building.

NATIONAL COPPER BANK BUILDING

Left: This 1911 photo shows the entrance to the National Copper Bank building. Because of a rash of bank robberies during the 1860s, banks toward the end of the century turned to elaborate safes to protect their customers' wealth. The designer of a bank would first address the specifications of the vault and then build the rest of the bank around it. Walls were typically one foot thick and doors were 3.5 feet thick—after all, thickness equated strength. *Below:* Vaults such as this one, shown in a 1910 photo, were typically made of reinforced concrete and metal.

Dapper folks pose in front of the New Grand Hotel and its free bus in July 1915. John C. Craig, the same architect who designed the Salt Lake Stock and Mining Exchange Building, the original Eagle Gate Apartments, and the Salt Lake Herald Building, designed the New Grand Hotel in 1910. Unlike the other Salt Lake buildings he designed, here Craig created a lively, colorful wall surface using terracotta tiles.

COMMERCIAL CLUB BUILDING

When businessmen who worked in the area needed to relax, meet socially, or gather for an informal business dinner, they would stroll across the plaza to the Commercial Club Building (pictured at right). Built in 1923, it is one of the most beautiful buildings in the city. Upon entering the building, the ceiling of the vestibule features images of buffalo heads and vegetation common in Utah. Although it currently serves as commercial space, for several years the building housed The Vortex, a dance club that featured floor-to-ceiling mirrors and go-go cages.

Below: The New Grand Hotel sits alongside the towering Boston and Newhouse buildings in 2009.
Bottom right: An elephant lamp illuminates the entrance of the Commercial Club Building.

FRANK E. MOSS FEDERAL COURTHOUSE

The 1902–1905 construction by the federal government of the Frank E. Moss Federal Courthouse (originally the U.S. Post Office and Courthouse) signaled that Salt Lake City and the state of Utah had survived the pioneer-era conflict with the government and had entered the 20th century.

Marking a permanent presence in the city, this monumental neoclassical revival–style building is anchored on Main Street by a distinct foundation not unlike a podium or platform that one would use to present a statue. The formality and rationality of the building's design seems fitting for an institution intended to perpetuate the rule of law, and it creates a distinctive physical and visual boundary to the nearby Exchange Place. Inside, the courtrooms feature elegant art deco glass, wood paneling, and decorative brass.

The courthouse has changed over the years since its inception: Additions have been added to the building twice, in 1910 and 1932. The tiled entryway once was the main public chamber of the post office. An interesting bas relief sculpture of a stylized eagle marks the entrance to the stairway leading to the building's main entrance, a familiar spot where news reporters confront defendants making their way out of court.

The Frank E. Moss Courthouse is shown here in 2008.

The second-story courtrooms have seen it all: A century of murder trials and fraud cases, as well as the trials in the wake of the infamous 2002 Winter Olympics bid scandal.

MARKET STREET

Toward the end of the 19th century, Salt Lake City was morphing from the original pioneer vision into a more complex tapestry of persons, politics, and economic activity. While LDS businesspeople tended to locate their companies near ZCMI at the top of Main Street, non-Mormons gravitated toward the Exchange Place district located near 400 South Main Street. Market Street is a small block dissecting Main Street and West Temple between 300 and 400 South.

After 1911, when the Union Pacific and Denver and Rio Grande railroad depots were built along 400 West, more than a dozen new hotels rose up in the downtown area, including the New York Hotel. Architect Richard K. A. Kletting designed the New York Hotel at 48 West Market Street for local entrepreneur Orange J. Salisbury, to be used for businessmen visiting Salt Lake City. The hotel's distinctive facade faced the Independent Order of Odd Fellows Hall built ten years earlier. The Independent Order of Odd Fellows (IOOF) represented that growing diversity, and they formed a non-Mormon counterpoint to the male priesthood of the LDS church.

Modern Market Street is known as a lively restaurant district offering some of the finest seafood in the Intermountain West, including the Market Street Grill and Oyster Bar, one of the premier restaurants in the Salt Lake Valley. Other notable restaurants, such as the New Yorker and Takashi, are a part of the diversity and range of settings and cuisines offered on Market Street.

The New York Hotel is shown above in 1906, and left, in 2009. A hotel for businesspeople in the early 20th century, today the New York Hotel has offices upstairs and three restaurants below. Each business is a part of Gastronomy Inc., a successful restaurant company known for its restoration and adaptive reuse of historic properties.

The Independent Order of Odd Fellows is a fraternal, benevolent, and social group that originated in England in the 18th century. Similar to freemasonry, it came to the United States in 1819 and grew in popularity with the population's movement into the western frontier and the country's industrialization. Above, club members pose in front of the building in 1911.

The Odd Fellows Hall is seen here in 1905. In the summer of 2009, the Odd Fellows Hall was moved to the other side of the street in a dramatic effort to save this important historic treasure and to make way for the expansion of the Frank Moss Courthouse.

Today, Market Street is a great place to find fine dining. The Market Street Grill and Oyster Bar is seen here in 2009.

The Rose Wagner Performing Arts Center is the site of many exciting performances by local groups and touring companies. For some, the most important activity that takes place in the theater auditorium is the Naturalization Ceremony for New American Citizens.

ROSE WAGNER PERFORMING ARTS CENTER

At the beginning of the 20th century, the area along West Broadway was alive with commercial activity, and the Wagner Bag Company was in the middle of it all. Such family businesses were built with hard work and business savvy. Harry and Rose Wagner—both immigrants to America—instilled in their children a respect for work, honesty, and community. With this upbringing, their son I. J. "Izzi" Wagner was primed for success. After Harry's death in 1932, Izzi, his

mother, and his brothers took over the family business. Together, they built a citywide empire of businesses.

Later in life, Wagner was the principal donor in building the Rose Wagner Performing Arts Center, named after his mother and built on the site of the original Wagner Bag Company. The center houses the Jeanné Wagner Theatre, named in honor of Wagner's late wife; and the Leona Wagner Black

Box Theatre, after his sister. The complex was built in phases, and the first portion opened in January 1996. This 150-seat "black box" theater with flexible seating cost $3 million and converts into two full rehearsal spaces complete with spring dance floors, dressing rooms, a green room, and the offices of the administrative staff. During the 2002 Winter Olympic Games, the *Tonight Show with Jay Leno* broadcasted live from the complex.

Actors Don Most (left) and Tom Hanks visit at the 2008 Sundance Film Festival. Since 1978, Sundance has become the largest independent film festival in the country. The "Rose" is an official venue of the festival.

Sunlight fills the spacious lobby at the Rose Wagner. Besides theaters and studio space, the center includes several permanent art installations, dance classes, and "Ring Around the Rose," an interactive activity especially for children.

The centerpiece to the complex is the Jeanné Wagner Theatre, a 500-seat auditorium that opened in March 2001. Built to the tune of $10.4 million, it is one of the most impressive performance venues in the region.

What was first known as the second Orpheum Theatre, but today as the Capitol Theatre, is nestled in between commercial buildings and the congestion of an urban street. This 1920 view shows traffic along 200 South near Main Street. The theater is on the far left.

CAPITOL THEATRE/SECOND ORPHEUM THEATRE

While it is difficult to imagine why Salt Lake City needed a second Orpheum, the next Orpheum Theatre opened in 1913 on 200 South just west of Main Street. Architect G. Albert Lansburgh of San Francisco (and schooled at the Paris Ecole des Beaux-Arts) imported national design styles and trends, creating one of the loveliest Italian renaissance revival–style buildings in town. The resulting theater indicated the city's growing sophistication and cultured citizenry.

The theater was widely hailed for its extravagant and lush interior decoration. Although it was constructed with the latest steel and reinforced-concrete technology, surface materials ranged from rich marble to lush carpets and drapery, mirrored reflectors, and glittering chandeliers. Between the first and second floors, a row of Palladian windows allowed ample natural sunlight. Vaudeville was all the rage at the time, and an impressive lineup of troupes and entertainers stopped in Salt Lake to perform at the theater, including Cowboy king Will Rogers, "red hot mama" Sophie Tucker, singer Trixie Friganza, and dancer-comedian Joe Frisco.

In 1927, the Louis Marcus chain bought and remodeled the theater to show motion pictures and changed the name to the Capitol Theatre. After 1976, the Salt Lake City Redevelopment Agency assumed ownership of the building. After another facelift, the theater's curtains rose once again in 1978. Today it is home to Ballet West and the Utah Opera.

This shot, taken during construction in 1912, captures the otherworldly nature of the Orpheum Theatre.

In 1927, the Orpheum became the Capitol Theatre. In this 1996 photo, the marquee advertises along "Broadway" (or rather, 200 South in downtown).

At right is a recent look inside the beautiful Capitol Theatre. When it was originally built, builders put in a "water curtain," or series of sprays in front of an asbestos curtain that activated when the temperature rose to a dangerous high. Even on the hottest day in August, a forced air system made it possible for audiences to attend performances and still be comfortable.

BICENTENNIAL ARTS COMPLEX

Salt Lake County dedicated the Bicentennial Arts Complex in September 1979. Architect Frank Ferguson designed the complex, containing the Symphony Hall and Salt Lake Art Center, in a modern abstract visual style. From the first, the music venue (renamed Abravanel Hall in 1993 for the Utah Symphony's longtime conductor Maestro Maurice Abravanel) was the core of a cluster of arts facilities that included the restored Capitol Theatre located around the corner.

Abravanel Hall is the home to the Utah Symphony, which was first organized in 1935. The building cuts a dramatic, diagonal swath in the downtown landscape southwest of Temple Square. Before one enters the symphony hall from the lobby, a sensational view of the cityscape is offered by a three-story curtain wall of tempered glass. The acoustical quality of the hall was based on exhaustive studies about optimum reverberation time and a mixture of tones and overtones.

Inside the Salt Lake Art Center, a grand staircase descends into the main gallery, one of the most elegant and exciting contemporary spaces in the city. According to the center's mission statement, the space exists to "encourage contemporary visual artists and art, which challenge and educate public perceptions of civil, social, and aesthetic issues affecting society." Like the contemporary art displayed within, the center is edgy, challenging the traditional grid of the city core and elevating the experience of art to a new level.

Top: The historic Salt Lake City Art Center building was at 59 South State Street. It was established in the 1930s by the Works Progress Administration (WPA). *Bottom:* Mahonri Young, grandson of Brigham Young, is perhaps best known for his sculpture *The Knockout,* for which he won the gold medal in sculpture in the 1932 Olympic Art Competition. Young's work is shown at the historic art center in this undated photo.

The dramatic geometry of the new Salt Lake Art Center's exterior (as seen here in 2008) captures the abstraction and avant-garde nature of the art typically exhibited within. The center's commitment to contemporary art, and its support of modern artists who move outside of traditional expressions, separates it from more mainstream local art venues.

SALT PALACE CONVENTION CENTER

There have been generations of iterations of the Salt Palace from the earliest site designed by architect Richard K. A. Kletting in 1899 on 900 South to the most recent incarnation on West Temple. Kletting was always one to tackle intriguing technical problems, but his innovative salt panels made of, well, salt, from the Great Salt Lake were more of an oddity than an engineering solution. The original building burned down in 1910; another Salt Palace center was built in 1969. After the Utah Jazz moved to play in the Delta Center, this building was demolished in 1994.

The current building, built in the mid-1990s and renamed the Calvin L. Rampton Salt Palace Convention Center in 2007, stretches two-thirds of the way along West Temple. Rejecting the traditional notion that a convention center's principal architectural identity is as a big box, the center is a marvel of sustainable green architecture. Twelve windmill sculptures lazily spin on the West Temple facade, the work of Montana artist Patrick Zentz. As they move, the windmills send electronically coded signals that set off 12 tonally different percussion instruments located in the convention center's

entrance tower atrium; the shifting patterns of seasons and the natural world blend and are reflected in sound. It's an acoustic feat that is confusing to some, but intriguing to others.

Above: Although the building itself was the focal point of the site, the land surrounding the unique Salt Palace was conceptualized as a public recreational spot complete with walking paths, a bicycle race track, a dance hall, and a theater. Here, a woman stands outside the Salt Palace circa 1900.

Left: Before the 1969 Salt Palace was demolished in 1994, it was the home to the Utah Jazz basketball team and various conventions that were held in the city. *Right:* The windmills running along the new Salt Palace are an example of the great potential for renewable energy in wind power—as well as a bit of whimsical entertainment.

Remodeled in 1995 for $80 million, the new Salt Palace (seen here in 2009) anticipated a significant jump in convention business for Salt Lake City. It also functioned as the media hub for the 2002 Winter Olympics.

ENERGYSOLUTIONS ARENA

Before the Delta Center (now EnergySolutions Arena) opened in 1991 in Salt Lake City's historic Gateway district, the Utah Jazz played basketball in the old Salt Palace on West Temple. Distinctive because of its diagonal orientation on the site, the center's glass-wall transparency exposes the excitement within. Crowds of people can be seen inside riding the escalators, pressing their way into entrances leading to the main arena, or standing in lines for concessions.

Salt Lake City–based firm FFKR Architects designed the space, earning an Award for Excellence in 1993. Frank Ferguson, senior partner at FFKR, described the building at night as "a giant urban lantern surrounded by heavily landscaped plazas." During the day, one can enjoy the Wasatch Mountains or downtown Salt Lake City reflected off the arena's ample window surfaces.

After Delta Airlines opted out in September 2006, EnergySolutions, a local low-level nuclear waste disposal company, bought the naming rights to the building. Much to the joy (or chagrin) of local sports fans, it is now known as the EnergySolutions Arena. The site sits on a ten-acre block near the Union Pacific Railroad Depot, the terminus of South Temple, and along 300 West. This proximity to downtown and the Gateway Mall place it at the center of Salt Lake City's vibrant urban activity.

The bronze statue of a basketball player stretching for a shot marks the home of the Utah Jazz—what was once known as the Delta Center and is now the EnergySolutions Arena.

THE 2002 WINTER OLYMPICS AT THE DELTA CENTER

More than 20,000 volunteers worked during the Olympic Games in February 2002 and an additional 6,000 for the Paralympic Winter Games that followed. Downtown, the Delta Center was the hub of the action. *Above:* The Delta Center is bedecked with the iconic Olympic rings, marking it as an official Olympic venue. *Bottom left:* Figure skater Sarah Hughes performs during the games. She went on to win a gold medal in the ladies' singles category.

THE PLACE TO BE

More than any other street in the city, South Temple illustrates Salt Lake City's transition from a dusty frontier town to a stratified urban environment with a certain degree of wealth. After 1870, mining entrepreneurs who extracted riches from Park City mines built extravagant mansions along South Temple. A variety of other buildings line South Temple as well, including carriage houses, churches, commercial and office buildings, a school, a hospital, medical clinics, clubhouses, and apartments. Over time, the street was transformed from a pioneer path into Salt Lake City's most glamorous boulevard, lined with the homes of some of the city's wealthiest citizens.

Originally surveyed as a graded dirt road on August 3, 1847, South Temple had a few hitching posts and not much else. But the city planners had a vision, and they incorporated road widths, land use, and density, much like what is seen in modern zoning. As time passed, additional features were found along the street, shaping it into a lovely and functional area: Uniform shade trees, light posts, stone curbs, masonry walls, and wrought-iron fences were all added to South Temple. Many of these historic elements still can be seen today.

HUMBLE BEGINNINGS

Brigham Young had envisioned that this east-west thoroughfare would serve the religious kingdom of Zion as a distinguished and prominent avenue in the heart of the city. In fact, South Temple

was commonly known as "Brigham Street" in its early years. Young took the lead by building residences for several of his wives here—the White House, the Log Row, the Beehive House, and the Lion House—as well as a tithing office and a school close to the church temple. Other city leaders followed suit and built their homes on South Temple as well, including church president Lorenzo Snow and LDS clerk and architect Hiram B. Clawson. By the beginning of the 20th century, however, several of these pioneer-era homes were replaced with apartments and men's clubs.

Despite Young's optimism, development of South Temple to the east was slow. Yet it was significant, in part because it provided a route to Red Butte Canyon, a ready source of red sandstone for con-

Although David and Mary Keith were at home in their exquisite mansion, which featured stained glass windows by Tiffany & Co. and a dazzling skylight in the rotunda, the newly wealthy and socially prominent Keiths did not entertain as much as their neighbors.

Left: The Kearns's South Temple home (seen here circa 1910) was easily one of the most elegant and extravagant residences in town.

struction, and later to Fort Douglas. South Temple was leveled and paved in the beginning of the 20th century; it remains an important connection between the University District and downtown. Today, South Temple breaks the pattern of the smaller lots found in the Avenues and the larger lots in Central City. Although a few mansions can be found south of South Temple (in the northern blocks of Central City), smaller, more modest homes built for middle-class families dominate the area.

The turn of the 19th century saw South Temple's largest building boom when several influential people—including wealthy mining, railroad, and commercial tycoons; senators; governors; mayors; and immigrant merchants—built their lavish homes there. The excellence of design and craftsmanship, and the diversity of architectural periods and styles, set this street apart. Utah's best craftspeople built their masterpieces on South Temple. Mining entrepreneur David Keith chose the neoclassical style for his family's South Temple mansion. Banking magnate Mathew Walker and his wife Angelena's second renaissance revival-style mansion was designed by the well-known local architectural firm of Ware & Treganza, while Richard K. A. Kletting designed the neoclassical mansion for

Enos Wall (that was used until 2008 as the LDS Business College Campus).

TO SEE AND BE SEEN

Society pages of the early 20th century often featured news about the wealthy—their parties, weddings, and extravagant travel plans—and nearly everything was deemed worth writing about. However, with the good came the bad, and scandals surfaced as well. Plenty of people talked when the Gardo House was built for Harriet Amelia Folsom, one of Young's youngest and prettiest wives, across the street from the Beehive House. Famous for her extravagant gowns and parties, Amelia flaunted her privileged position while Young's other wives lived far more modestly. Later, Susanna Bransford Emery Holmes Delitch Engalitcheff, dubbed "Utah's Silver Queen," lived in the Gardo House with her husband (the second of four), where they were known for their parties. In 1926, Gardo House was torn down and replaced with the Federal Reserve Bank.

Clubhouses provided a place to be seen, gather, and socialize. So it seemed only appropriate that the Alta Club, Elks Club, Ladies Literary Club, and the Masonic Temple were all located along South Temple near the homes of their wealthy members. The Elks Club constructed its club headquarters in 1923 and was a popular national fraternal organization among Salt Lake City's non-Mormon community. The Ladies Literary Club, founded in 1877, played an important role in the development of

At the Anniversary Inn (the former Kahn Mansion), visitors can stay in a number of exotic themed rooms, including this Mysteries of Egypt suite.

A HISTORICAL STREET

Non-Mormons came to Utah following the cache of precious metals surfacing in Utah in the latter half of the 19th century. The construction of the First Presbyterian Church in 1906 and the Cathedral of the Madeleine in 1909 proved that increasing numbers of Presbyterians and Catholics were settling down in Mormon-dominated Utah. The decision of these two religions to locate their most significant buildings on South Temple alongside the Mormon Temple marked a coming-of-age for the additional religious communities and congregations in Utah.

Finally, with the introduction of income taxes in 1913, individual wealth began to shrink and retaining single-family mansions was no longer practical. Moreover, zoning changes in the 1920s permitted commercial development along South Temple, and the area saw a higher density development than in the past. Demolition of 30 of the 40 grand mansions at mid-century contributed to the decline of the street. However, because of its outstanding historical and architectural significance, South Temple was designated Salt Lake City's first historic district in 1975. South Temple is an eloquent reminder of a particular moment in Utah's history: when mines promised great wealth, and rich entrepreneurs lived lavishly, expressed through the city's housing and commercial architecture.

public libraries in Utah and other philanthropic projects.

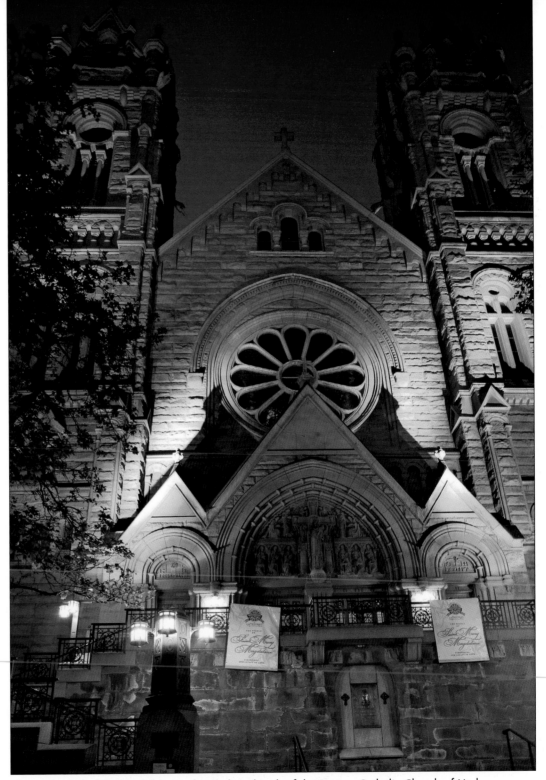

The Cathedral of the Madeleine is the mother church of the Roman Catholic Church of Utah. Rededicated in 1993, visitors and worshippers can enjoy recitals and programs throughout the year hosted by the Cathedral of the Madeleine and the Madeleine Choir School.

EAGLE GATE

Over the years, three versions of the Eagle Gate have expanded across State Street at South Temple. Brigham Young built the first Eagle Gate in 1859 to stand as the formal entrance to his family estate at the mouth of City Creek Canyon. Surrounded by a nine-foot-tall wall, Young's estate included two ample adobe brick homes, a schoolhouse, orchards, and vegetable gardens in the back.

The original gate was 22 feet wide—quite a difference compared to the third and current version that spans 76 feet across State Street. Ralph Ramsey, a talented local woodworker, carved the original gate's iconic eagle. Today, this wooden eagle sits on display at the Daughters of Utah Pioneers Museum on Main Street across from the Capitol building.

The city erected the third Eagle Gate in 1963 after a truck damaged the previous gate beyond repair. For this incarnation, a hefty bronze eagle with a 20-foot wingspan was made to perch on top of the gate, presiding over South Temple. The gate continues to serve as a stately entrance into the city and particularly (after the turn of the century) the street leading up to the Utah State Capitol.

In 1882, State Street opened as a thoroughfare through the Eagle Gate—a threshold to the northern part of the city—which significantly increased traffic. Before long, it became obvious that to accommodate the traffic from horse-drawn carriages and trolley cars (as seen here in 1904), a new, larger gate was needed. As a result, in 1891, the second Eagle Gate was erected, designed by Brigham Young's son Joseph Don Carlos Young.

The Eagle Gate has witnessed the transformation of transportation from the horse-drawn buggy (such as this one in the early 20th century) to the latest hybrid autos available today.

ALICE MERRILL HORNE

As a pioneer entering the Salt Lake Valley in the 1840s, Alice Merrill Horne's mother carried her carefully packed paints and brushes across the Rocky Mountain range. Clearly, Horne was primed for her future role as Utah's "First Lady of the Arts." When she was 23 years old she was chosen as chairwoman of the Utah Liberal Arts Committee for the 1893 Columbian Exposition in Chicago, publishing an accompanying book of poems by Utah women. Seven years later, Horne was the second woman to be elected to the Utah House of Representatives, where she pushed for legislation impacting the arts. She is perhaps best known for backing a bill to create what would be the first art institute in the country, as well as founding annual art exhibits and the first state art collection. As a member of the LDS church's General Board of National Women's Relief Society, Horne helped write lessons on the arts, architecture, and landscapes, and even wrote articles for various LDS publications.

But Horne was progressive in other matters as well. At the turn of the century, she and a group of local women staged a sit-in at the base of the Brigham Young monument to protest the terrible pollution generated by coal-burning stoves, furnaces, and factories. In a dramatic demonstration of just how bad the conditions were, the women—dressed entirely in white, from white feather boas and hats to elegant white gowns—dragged the fingers of their gloved hands along the base of the statue and held them up in the air, demonstrating the amount of dirt and grime that was epidemic throughout the city.

Eagle Gate (seen at top circa 1967; above, a closer look at the iconic eagle in 1996) frames a dramatic view of the Utah State Capitol. In 1983, State Street was the scene of spring runoff floods. Sand bags lined State Street for weeks before the water abated. Then-Governor Scott M. Matheson's comment, "This is a hell of a way to run a desert," captured the essence of the contrast the abundant water made with the region's typically arid climate.

ALTA CLUB

In 1883, an exclusive, non-Mormons-only men's organization opened called the Alta Club—a testament to the community's deep religious divide. Named after the Alta mining district in Little Cottonwood Canyon, the original club members had strong ties to the mining industry. Touting both economic wealth and political influence in the city and territory, these original 81 men were definitely the "Who's Who" of the local non-Mormon community. In fact, many were multimillionaires. The original Alta Club was located in the Alta Block at 21 West 200 South; several years later, the club moved to its current location at 100 East South Temple.

A couple of years after the club's inception, Mormons were allowed membership, marking improved relations between the two groups. More importantly, the change revealed new realities: The city's economic landscape was more complex and depended on the goodwill of businesspeople regardless of their religious backgrounds. More than 100 years later, in 1987, the club repealed its ban on nonwidowed female members. In 2007, Ceri Jones was elected the Alta Club's first female president.

The club has seen its share of famous people and infamous incidences. In 1923, the author of the Sherlock Holmes mystery series, Sir Arthur Conan Doyle, and his wife spoke at a luncheon given at the Alta Club during an American lecture tour. And during the Prohibition era, Alta Club members often brought their own liquor, having met their bootlegger down the street at the Hotel Utah to pick up deliveries. In this way, members were able to avoid any embarrassment to the Alta Club in the event police officers were to intervene and make an arrest.

While the Alta Club's membership eventually included Mormons, it was a century before women were allowed to join. Before then, ladies came as guests but had to enter through a special entrance reserved for women at the back of the building to the west. The Alta Club is seen here at its current location in 1905.

In 2001, the Alta Club completed a $4.2 million restoration of the building. Many of the club's historic features remain, such as these stained glass windows.

THE CATHEDRAL OF THE MADELEINE

In 1776, Fathers Francisco Antanasio Dominguez and Silvestre Velez de Escalante traveled through Utah on their way to Santa Fe. The two men were in search of a trade route and locations for new missions for Spain and the Catholic Church. These early visitors to the territory brought with them the first regional Catholic missionaries in what would become the American West and Utah Territory.

Bishop Lawrence Scanlon arrived in Salt Lake City in 1873 as a 30-year-old seminarian from Ireland. At the time of his arrival, there were only 90 Catholics in Salt Lake City and nearby Ogden combined. Even so, he was ready for the challenge of converting Mormons. Scanlon purchased the land in 1890 for $30,000, but building the Cathedral of the Madeleine became a long process, completed in 1909. Designed by architect Carl M. Neuhausen, the exterior features round arches and rough-cut stone and is an excellent example of the Romanesque style popular at the time. Neuhausen died before the cathedral was finished, so Bernard O. Mecklenberg was hired to finish the roof and towers, which are adorned with gargoyles. Originally, the interior was plain, but thanks to the work of famed architect John Comes, who infused it with an ornate Spanish Gothic style featuring bright and vivid colors, today the cathedral is anything but dull.

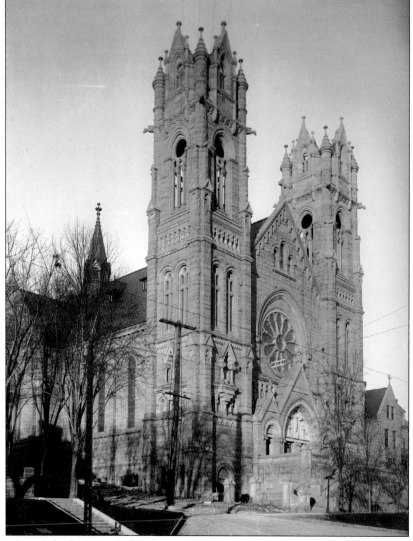

Above left: The bas relief sculpture of the recessed arch area over the central entrance is familiar cathedral iconography: Jesus Christ is flanked on both sides by the apostles. The church's Gothic pointed arches, rusticated stone, and elaborately modulated wall surface locate the building in a long tradition of cathedral architecture, what the artist Auguste Rodin called "the scaffolding of heaven." *Above:* The eight gargoyles projecting out from the corners of the uppermost point of the roof (as seen here in the early 20th century) were built in 1917. By 1930, the gargoyles had eroded into nothing. In September 1977, a crane lifted new versions of the tremendously heavy sculptures—weighing 1,200 pounds each—into place at the top of the 150-foot towers.

INSIDE THE MADELEINE

Since its dedication in 1909, the cathedral has been the site for Catholics to worship, pray, mourn, and celebrate. *Above:* In this photo from 1941, a ceremony at the Cathedral of the Madeleine is held for graduating nurses. *Right:* Among the many standout features of the cathedral are the enormous stained glass windows representing the apostles and the mysteries of the rosary; the 14 stations of the cross, painted by University of Utah professor Roger (Sam) Wilson in 1992 and 1993; and this dual-level baptismal font. The font, dedicated in 1993, features Carrara onyx and a delicately ornate glass mosaic.

FIRST PRESBYTERIAN CHURCH

In 1871, Reverend Josiah Welch arrived in Utah. He was one of the Presbyterian missionaries that were coming to the state with the advent of the railroad, and Corinne, a railroad town to the north of Salt Lake City, was their home. Within a short period of time, there was a significant presence of these missionaries in Salt Lake City as well. Welch amassed a small congregation—initially just 12 members.

For some years, the First Presbyterian Church moved from building to building to accommodate its growing number of worshippers. Finally, the local congregation was able to raise the funds needed to build a church at the corner of South Temple and C Street. The cornerstone was laid in 1903, and the construction of the First Presbyterian Church building proved they were there to stay.

The church was designed in a Gothic revival-style by local Utah architect Walter E. Ware. Modeled after the Carlisle Cathedral in Carlisle, England, the church was constructed of red sandstone that was quarried in Red Butte and transported to the city on rail lines. The church was dedicated on May 12, 1906. Five months later, a storm blew out the incredible east window that depicted the first Easter. The congregation raised more than $3,000 for its replacement. First Presbyterian is known for its other stained glass artwork as well: The west window depicts Jesus's birth, while the south window shows Jesus at Gethsemane.

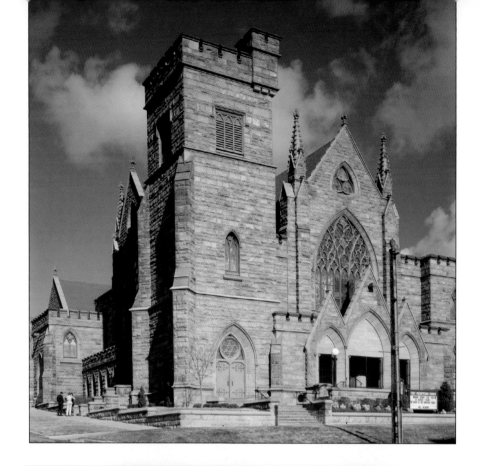

Top: In 2000, the church (seen here circa 2008) underwent a restoration project; during this time, the three large stained glass windows were dismantled, cleaned, and reassembled. *Bottom:* The First Presbyterian church choir is shown here in 1907.

In 1903, the Kearns Mansion was lavishly decorated inside and out to welcome President Theodore Roosevelt to Salt Lake City.

KEARNS MANSION/GOVERNOR'S MANSION

Thomas Kearns arrived in Utah in 1883, a poor 21-year-old immigrant. Within a few years he was a partner in the Silver King Mining Company, a venture that enabled him to become one of the wealthiest and most influential men in the state. Besides his mining activities, Kearns was also co-owner of *The Salt Lake Tribune* and served in the U.S. Senate from 1901 to 1905.

Such an ambitious man deserved an ambitious home. Architect Carl

Neuhausen designed this magnificent house at 603 East South Temple for the Kearns in 1902. The French chateau-style home features extravagant details including French moiré silk wall coverings and hand-cut marble mosaic flooring. The library has a black Flemish oak floor that adds a striking contrast to the African red marble fireplace. Beautiful woodwork, plastering, murals and stenciling, crystal chandeliers, and countless other elaborate details made the house a real showplace.

In 1937, Jennie donated the home for use as Utah's first official governor's residence, but in 1957 the state legislature funded the construction of a new governor's residence in the Federal Heights area. The mansion became a governor's residence once again in 1980; Governor Olene Walker lived there briefly, as well as three other former governors. Most recently, Governor Jon Huntsman and his family have resided in the mansion.

Thomas and Jennie Kearns had three children who grew up in the 32-room mansion. The family spent countless hours in the bowling alley (seen here in 1907) in the basement, where they set up the pins by hand and kept score on a chalkboard. It is said that they also owned two trouble-making monkeys from South America for a time. There was plenty of room for entertainment elsewhere in the house as well, including a ballroom, two parlors, and two dining rooms.

Left and above: A devastating fire on December 15, 1993, sparked by defective Christmas lights, destroyed much of the interior of the Kearns (now Governor's) Mansion. The elegant central, circular staircase, one of the most architecturally distinctive features of the building, worked against itself here, sweeping heat and smoke up toward the central roof dome and damaging it beyond repair. A restoration, completed in July 1996, brought the gem back to its original glory. Today (as seen here), the mansion still sparkles with vintage charm.

THE MANSIONS

Some of Salt Lake City's finest residences can be found along South Temple. The area attracted the wealthy, who spared no expense on their lavish mansions. As a whole, the homes are architecturally distinctive, extravagantly detailed, and a fine representation of wealth—as well as a sign of the growing stratification of Salt Lake society at the time.

Some of the mansions are pictured here, but there were plenty of other grandiose residences on South Temple. Enos Wall, cofounder of the Utah Copper Company in Bingham Canyon, built a mansion at 411 East South Temple that featured such details as gilded frescoes and seven fireplaces. Built in 1881 and remodeled by Richard K. A. Kletting, this now-empty residence once housed the Salt Lake Jewish Center, the Pacific National Life Insurance Company, and the LDS Business College.

After becoming president of the Walker Brothers Bank (as well as one of the richest men in Utah), Mathew Walker and his wife Angelena hired the architectural firm Ware & Treganza to design their second renaissance revival–style mansion. Built in 1904 at 610 East South Temple, the mansion included a grand hall that contained a massive organ with 1,500 pipes that extended to the third floor. The mansion has served as an office space since 1943.

The over-the-top carriage house of David and Mary Keith (above, in 1966), not only housed the servants, but also had a bowling alley and shooting gallery.

A group of society ladies take an afternoon drive past the Glendinning Mansion in 1909. Salt Lake Mayor James Glendinning lived in his mansion, built in 1883 at 617 East South Temple, with his wife, Margaret, and their children. Unfortunately, Glendinning's term in office was plagued by personal and political scandal, including a struggle with alcoholism.

Left: A staircase in the historic Glendinning Mansion (left, in 2009) winds upward (or is it down?). The mansion has changed hands several times over the years. Today it is home to the main offices of the Utah Arts Council, as well as the Alice Gallery, named after Utah's "First Lady of the Arts," Alice Merrill Horne.

AN ENCHANTED LIFE

Built in 1889, the Queen Anne–style Kahn Mansion (shown above left in 1966) features a polygonal turret and carved gingerbread detailing. The Kahn Brothers, Emanuel and Samuel, owned what became the largest produce market in the city and were among Utah's first Jewish immigrants. A trustee of the B'nai Israel Synagogue and a leader in the community, Emanuel died on January 31, 1905. It's a good bet that the Kahn brothers wouldn't recognize the interior of the house today. Now the mansion is the site of the Anniversary Inn. At bottom right is one of the inn's themed rooms, the Enchanted Forest.

SALT LAKE MASONIC TEMPLE

The discovery of King Tutankhamen's tomb in 1922 led to the widespread popularity of Egyptian revival architecture. Local architects Carl W. Scott and George W. Welch used this style when they designed the Salt Lake Masonic Temple. Included in the design are many Egyptian symbols as well as motifs significant to the Masons, appearing in inscriptions and bas-relief sculptures.

Built in 1927, the temple features eight lotus columns that support a curved cornice featuring a carving of Horus, the Egyptian god of light and life. The center of this work features Masonic symbols, such as an Egyptian sun disk with the Masonic square, compass, and the letter "G." Flanking the entrance are two sphinxes made of Utah granite, signifying great strength and intelligence, between whose paws are granite spheres that represent the Celestial Sphere and Terrestrial Sphere—the intersection of heaven and earth.

The temple is three stories high, embodying the three degrees of Masonry. Visitors enter by climbing three staircases of five, seven, and nine steps, respectively—combinations that represent the number of rungs found in the storied Jacob's ladder reaching to heaven. The temple houses a 1,400-seat auditorium featuring a ceiling painted with the star constellations of the universe, as well as a public library, banquet hall, meeting rooms, and administrative offices.

The first Masonic Temple (above), built in 1905, eventually proved too small a space for the increasing number of members.

The entire temple is covered in symbols rife with meaning to Masons, including the sphinxes (left) and at the entrance (above). Describing the utmost importance placed on secrecy, architect Carl W. Scott drolly noted, "Legend tells us that rulers in the past often blinded or put to death their builders upon completion of their work, that they might not disclose the secret wine vault or do a better job for another client. Naturally, the author does not look with favor upon such a practice."

THE LADIES LITERARY CLUB

The Ladies Literary Club was established in 1877, but it was 35 years before the construction of their clubhouse at 850 East South Temple. Conceived as a club for women who loved literature and had a desire to learn, many of the members were writers themselves. The Ladies Literary Club was an offshoot of an earlier, far more exclusive organization called The Blue Tea that gave local socialites a chance to gather for intellectual and social activity.

The Ladies Literary Club, however, had a different agenda. It was and still is recognized for its charitable work to expand the cultural and educational life of the city, including its role in the development of libraries in Utah. Not only did the club support the Mason's public library, but it also supported the passage of a bill to fund the state's first library, which passed in 1896. The club's inaugural president, Mrs. J. C. Role, once said of the group, "As an infant the Club was most ambitious. We essayed great things—We were, indeed, a most precocious infant."

The club building was designed in 1912 by the architectural firm Ware & Treganza. It is still considered to be one of Utah's finest examples of Prairie-style architecture. During World War I, the women set up sewing machines in the clubhouse auditorium; on Wednesdays members spent the day making children's clothes and hospital clothes for disabled veterans. Through both World Wars and into the current century, the women continue to provide their devoted service in this building.

For a number of years, the Ladies Literary Club was rather nomadic. The group met first in private homes and then in a series of buildings, including this house at 43 East Fifth Street (top, seen here at the turn of the 20th century) and their first clubhouse (bottom, in 1910) located at 20 South 300 East in 1898. When it was founded, the Ladies Literary Club was the first of 12 of its kind in the country, and the first west of the Mississippi River. Utah women had already had the vote for seven years, and members were energetically engaged in a range of philanthropic endeavors.

Right: In 1897, Ladies Literary Club President Eurithe K. LaBarthe, a member of Utah's first State Legislature, helped pass the "High Hat Bill," which made the wearing of high hats by women illegal—because the hats blocked the view of fellow theatergoers. In this photo, members dress up (in modest hats, no less) to celebrate the club's centennial in 1977.

Left and above: The club's permanent home at 850 East South Temple was built in 1913. The Ladies Literary Club offered "sections" that gave members the chance to meet in smaller groups around shared interests, such as Book Chat, Bridge, Drama-Music, History-Tourist, and Civic Affairs. Members would attend the general club meeting once a month as well as a section meeting.

HAXTON PLACE

Haxton Place deviates from Salt Lake City's usual grid plan by creating a type of pocket off South Temple. This half-block-long residential cul-de-sac runs along the south side of the street and includes some of the most architecturally distinctive houses in the district. Purchased in 1909 by local dentist James T. Keith, he left the designing of Haxton Place to Thomas G. Griffin, an Englishman who modeled the area after Haxton Place in London.

Frederick A. Hale designed the Keith and Griffin houses, the first residences to be built in Haxton Place. What appears to be a duplex at the south end of the street is actually two houses built about 17 inches apart. The Keith and Griffin families shared this lot and a tennis court that was built behind the two homes, which also share a Tudor revival-style sensibility.

Restrictive covenants were put into place when Haxton Place was created to ensure that only "first class" residences would be constructed. Not only did the covenants dictate that these homes had to cost more than $5,000 to construct, but they went a step further—and only because Keith owned the district could these covenants have been in place—and stated that if a person of Chinese or African descent purchased a house, the building would automatically revert back to the original owner. The photo above shows a Haxton area residence in 1910.

Across the street from Haxton Place is Haxton Manor, an English-style inn, seen here in 2009.

The Avenues

NEIGHBORHOOD ON THE HILL

As the first area of the city to deviate from the original pioneer plan of ten-acre plots, the Avenues was destined to be unique. Even today the Avenues district continues to showcase its diversity in both its residents and architecture. With smaller blocks and narrower streets than those found downtown and houses nestled close to the street, this neighborhood manifests itself as densely intimate, with a similar feel to row houses found on the East Coast.

As was the custom in the city's core, originally the streets in the Avenues were named rather than numbered. It wasn't until 1907 that the city council changed the names of streets to the alphabetical street names (A Street to Virginia Street) and numbered avenues (1st to 18th Avenue) that we know today.

Prior to 1880, this area was sparsely populated due to lack of water, but soon the city found a way to exploit City Creek, which flowed from the mountains into the Jordan River. The city diverted the stream into a ditch that ran along Fourth Avenue, providing potable and irrigation water. Moreover, through a system of head gates and ditches, City Creek provided water to different parts of the town and acted as its main water source until 1879. In fact, City Creek proved integral to the building of Salt Lake City, powering Utah's first mill in 1847. Soon the stream was used for operating local sawmills, gristmills, a turning mill, and a cording mill.

With water came the people. First platted in 1854, by 1889 the Avenues became a popular residential area. Convenient and accessible to downtown, local amenities, such as markets and shopping, added to the appeal. For decades, the Eighth Avenue Meat and Grocery has been a neighborhood anchor. Gibson's Tailor Shop could be found at the corner of Q Street and Second Avenue; today it is the home to Q Street Fine Crafts. The 20th Ward Store was located on Fourth Avenue.

In this photo from 1907, men work to put in new sidewalks and streets in the Avenues, a neighborhood that continued to expand to the north and east.

Left: This 2009 view from above the Federal Heights neighborhood and the Avenues running along Virginia Street to the east gives a great vantage point of the city and a profound sense of the curvature of the mountains.

Smith's on Sixth Avenue and E Street has long served as the "modern" grocery store for the neighborhood. In 1860, the slaughteryards moved from 800 South and State Street to the East Bench near the mouth of Dry Canyon to take advantage of the ready supply of water there. Since the men that worked in the slaughteryards also lived there, the eastern end of the Avenues became known as Butcherville. Today the area is known as Federal Heights, one of the most exclusive neighborhoods in Salt Lake City.

Trolley rails also contributed to the settlement of the neighborhood. By 1872, the Salt Lake Railway Company offered horse- and mule-drawn trolley services through the area. In 1889, the trolleys went electric, running up Third, Sixth, and Ninth Avenues, which are wider and flatter than the surrounding roads. At one time there were several different competing rail lines servicing the area. By the 1940s, the trolleys disappeared when automobiles replaced public transportation.

IT TAKES A VILLAGE

But shops and residences don't entirely make up a community. Churches, schools, and a hospital also helped shape the Avenues. The historic LDS Hospital, opened January 5, 1905, was built on Eighth Avenue, high above the hustle and bustle of the city. Today, the hospital is immersed in the Avenues neighborhood. Starting with five stories, 80 small patient rooms, and a fancy new X-ray machine, the building has gone through a number of phases. Now, with about 5,000 employees and years of alterations and additions, the hospital's original builders probably would not recognize it.

The oldest private school in the state, the Rowland Hall-Saint Mark's School campus on First Avenue originally began as two separate Episcopal schools: St. Mark's coed school (founded in 1867) and Rowland Hall, a boarding school for girls (1880). In 1964, the two merged to become a college prep school. As the area grew in popularity, so did the school; in 1984, middle and high school students were moved to a renovated location on Lincoln Street. In 2002, yet another campus opened for the school's youngest students on Guardsman Way near the University of Utah campus. While the school is no longer affiliated with the Episcopal church, this cluster of school buildings represents an important phase in Utah's educational and religious history: The Episcopal church, although never a majority religion in Utah, was one of the first non-Mormon denominations to send clergy to the area to provide community, religious, and educational services for church members.

ARCHITECTS FOR HIRE

With the growth of Park City and other Utah mining communities came wealth. And with money and growth came work for professional architects. Several prominent turn-of-the-century architects built or rented homes in the Avenues: Richard K. A. Kletting, Walter E. Ware, Albert O. Treganza, Frederick A. Hale, and Lewis Telle Cannon all designed homes in the Avenues.

Led by their prophet and colonizer Brigham Young, the Mormon pioneers settled the Salt Lake Valley after making the long trek from Nauvoo, Illinois. Some of those who lost their lives are honored here at the Mormon Pioneer Memorial.

Memory Grove Park (shown here in recent times) was formally dedicated on June 27, 1924, as a war memorial park to Utah's fallen servicemen.

The late 19th century saw an increase in rental housing, and in the first two decades of the 20th century, there was a movement toward speculative properties and subdivisions. Of the nine officially platted subdivisions, Darlington Place (located between N and S Streets and First and Third Avenues) stands as a good example of this trend. Developers and builders also contributed to the area with pattern-book homes, and larger apartments began to appear interspersed between family homes. Although most apartment buildings are of simple, straightforward designs, there are some great examples of architectural styles applied to larger buildings. One of the best art moderne-style apartments in the city is the Wymer located on First Avenue. The Hillcrest Apartments, also on First Avenue, includes large U-shaped blocks that balance enough open space with the structure to give it a residential feel.

The Avenues experienced a significant decline between the Great Depression years of the 1930s through the mid-1960s. Families fled city living for subdivisions to the south, and several building owners divided single-family homes into apartment units. Absentee landlords were abundant. It wasn't until the late 1960s that there was neighborhood revitalization and whole blocks of historic homes were restored to their original beauty.

Although the Avenues is one of Salt Lake City's oldest neighborhoods, its vitality and progressive, artsy vibe makes it feel as though it is the youngest. Today the Avenues is one of the most sought-after places to live in the city.

CITY CREEK

The mouth of City Creek Canyon was one of the early campsites used by the Mormon pioneers when they arrived in the valley in 1847. The stream that flows through the canyon and into the city below continues to provide a valuable and reliable water source to residents of Salt Lake City.

The pioneers wasted little time upon their arrival. Within days, the water was dammed and diverted to form irrigation ditches, including a canal that ran west along North Temple. Water from these diversions and reservoirs in upper City Creek continues to supply parts of Salt Lake City. The city diverted the lower City Creek into an underground culvert in 1909, and they developed the filled-in creek bed into median park areas along Canyon Road. Pioneer leaders recognized the immense value in City Creek and exploited it to provide industrial power and operate various mills.

By the 1880s, houses sprang up around the base of City Creek Canyon, significantly changing the character of the neighborhood. The residential neighborhood continues to thrive today, nourishing its residents in this green urban landscape just outside of town.

With such close proximity to town, Canyon Road proved to be an ideal location to live with a variety of housing types, such as these apartments shown on the far right in 1908. The street continues to be residential. It's not uncommon to see people walking or riding their bikes to and from the neighborhood.

Early on, the city diverted City Creek underground as it brought water to different parts of Salt Lake City. This photo shows the City Creek Aqueduct at North Temple and 400 West in 1909.

George M. Ottinger, the city's first paid fire chief, led the Veterans Volunteer Firemen's Association for 27 years. During his leadership, in 1900 Ottinger Hall (seen here in 1996) was built. In 2004, the city matched the Salt Lake City Rotary Foundation's donation of $100,000 toward the renovation of Ottinger Hall. When the work was complete, YouthCity moved into the building, providing after-school and summer activities and classes for local youth.

THE 1999 TORNADO

ALTHOUGH SALT LAKE CITY certainly has the right conditions for tornadoes—dry air and a location within a bowl-like valley contained by mountain ranges—rarely does the phenomenon actually occur. On August 11, 1999, history was made when an F2-level tornado ravaged its way through downtown Salt Lake City. Within a short time, the twister touched down, resulting in one death, 80 injuries, and more than $170 million in damages.

Before the disaster, in the early morning a warm and breezy southerly wind rushed through the valley. By noon it was clear that a convergence zone had developed—vertical shearing of the winds marked by different wind speeds, the jet-stream over northern Utah, and thunderstorms over the Oquirrh Mountains to the west. At 12:35 P.M., the conditions culminated in a huge and powerful thunderstorm, and clouds as high as 41,000 feet produced an F2 tornado. The storm caused significant damage at the Delta Center and uprooted hundreds of trees in Memory Grove and along the way up the Avenues. In total, it traveled four and a quarter miles and vertically moved 1,095 feet— all within 14 minutes.

In an arid environment such as the Salt Lake Valley, readily accessible water could make or break a fledgling settlement. The town appointed water masters who fairly distributed City Creek's waters in order to redeem and enrich the dry landscape. Although some citizens dug their own wells, far more relied on city canal systems and ditches that ran parallel to just about every street in town. Throughout Utah's history, the effort required to locate and divert adequate water supplies has been endemic. Utah's irrigation efforts were models for the redemption of arid lands throughout the region. The lush greenery around City Creek Park in downtown Salt Lake City (seen here in 1996) is proof of the pioneers' success.

MEMORY GROVE PARK

In 1902, the city purchased land in lower City Creek with the intent to use it as a public park. It wasn't until after World War I, however, that it actually became a park. Thanks to the efforts of the Service Star Legion women, who had the area dedicated as Memory Park, the land was transformed from a wild canyon into a beautiful veteran's memorial. The park is home to the Meditation Chapel and the Memorial House. Other monuments were added later, such as the Harbor of Beauty, a pond that was dedicated in memory of sailors who died while serving their country.

What is now known as the Memorial House was built circa 1890 to be used as a stable and storage shed for the P. J. Moran Company. The city took over the barn when the land was purchased, and for a time it served as a tool shed and black-smith shop. The Service Star group leased it from the city in 1926, and they hired the local architectural firm Pope & Burton to design a new facade. Until the 1980s, the building was used as a reception and events center. After standing vacant for ten years, the Memorial House once again operates as an events center, and it is now home to the Utah Heritage Foundation.

Mr. and Mrs. Ross Beason built the Meditation Chapel in 1948 to serve as a memorial to their son and other soldiers who died during World War II. Made of Georgia marble, this small chapel has large bronze doors and four stained glass windows representing the four branches of the armed forces.

Above: Designed by architect Slack Winburn, the Pagoda was the first monument built in Memory Grove Park and is made from the same marble as the Lincoln Memorial in Washington, D.C. *Above left:* The entrance gates, also designed by Winburn, bear the name "Memory Park," as the park was originally known. It wasn't until the late 1960s that the park became known as Memory Grove Park. Both photos were taken in the 1940s.

The 1948 dedication of Meditation Chapel (seen here in recent times) boasts the largest number of people—an estimated 20,000—to visit the park at one time.

More than 300 granite markers (some shown here in 2009) are found in the plaza in front of the chapel, representing the Utah servicemen whose remains were never recovered during World War II.

Although the Memorial House (seen here in 2009) has changed considerably from its original brick structure, there still remain clues to its former life: double doors for a hay loft were later replaced by a double window above the main entry.

BRIGHAM YOUNG GRAVESITE

Befitting a man who was the president and prophet of a church, the governor of a territory, and the uniquely talented colonizer of the Great Basin Kingdom, Brigham Young has his own cemetery within the Mormon Pioneer Park. The space is reserved for his grave and the graves of some of his favorite wives: Eliza R. Snow Smith, Mary Angell Young, and Lucy A. D. Young, as well as his daughter Alice Young Clawson and eldest son, Joseph A. Young.

When Brigham died in 1877 at age 76, it was the end of an era. His life spanned the era of LDS church founder Joseph Smith, the exodus to the American West, and the settlement of Utah Territory. Many family members were present at his deathbed, including Zina Presendia Young Williams (Brigham's daughter with Zina Diantha Young, a widow of Joseph Smith's), who commented, "He seemed to partially revive, and opening his eyes, he gazed upward, exclaiming: 'Joseph, Joseph, Joseph' and the divine look in his face seemed to indicate that he was communicating with Joseph Smith, the Prophet."

Rather than a grand monument attesting to his enormous regional influence, Brigham's grave is marked by a simple headstone surrounded by a small cast-iron fence, as seen here in this turn-of-the-century photo. The site is a quiet element on First Avenue, a block away from the Beehive and Lion houses.

Church leader Daniel H. Wells spoke at Brigham's funeral: "I arise with an aching heart, but cannot let pass this opportunity of paying at least a tribute of respect to our departed friend and brother, who has just stepped behind the veil. I can only say, let the silent tears fall that it may give relief to the troubled heart; for we have lost our counselor, our friend, our president....Goodbye, Brother Brigham until the morning of the resurrection day, when thy lifelong companions who will soon follow after will me[e]t thee in peace and joy." A bust of Brigham is seen at right.

caption to come

SALT LAKE CITY CEMETERY

Situated just northeast of the city in the Avenues district and looking south over the valley, the 250-acre Salt Lake City Cemetery is the largest city-owned cemetery in the entire country. Approximately 120,000 people are buried here, including many religious and political leaders such as Mormon architect Truman O. Angell and state senators Frank Moss and Wallace Bennett.

The first burial took place in September 1847, a couple months after the Mormon pioneers had settled the valley. In 1851, Salt Lake City was incorporated, and the first 20 acres surveyed for burial grounds officially became the Salt Lake City Cemetery. The layout of the cemetery follows the grid pattern found in the rest of the city, repeating the ordered and practical rationality of these early pioneers.

Cemeteries showcase the stories of the men and women whose lives are commemorated in simple headstones and the symbols families think best sum up their lives. The Salt Lake City Cemetery suggests various social realities, including relationships between plural families, sweeping illnesses (such as the Spanish Flu), and the eras of various wars.

Above left: The Salt Lake City Cemetery tells a larger story than just that of the Mormon settlers. The cemetery also reflects the city and its various groupings of ethnicities and beliefs, as well as the story of the origins of the state of Utah: There is a Catholic section of the cemetery, as well as Jewish, Chinese, and Japanese sections. There's even a section for the prospectors who died en route to California. *Above right:* Two 19th-century tombstones succinctly sum up the lives of two local residents.

In this photo, two gentlemen drive through the entrance to Federal Heights in March 1909. Moving toward the more natural and organic configuration that would become typical of American suburbs, Federal Heights represented a certain version of the good life—abundant landscaping and natural streetscapes, open space, and formal elements such as this stone entrance into the subdivision. Acting as a threshold into the more extravagant neighborhood to the east, the pillars form a boundary between social classes and clearly mark the border surrounding an architecturally and socially distinct neighborhood of the city.

FEDERAL HEIGHTS

A fellow named Charles Popper was the first settler to claim land and establish his home in the area now known as Federal Heights. Popper, a cattle rancher and butcher, purchased the property shortly after arriving in Utah in 1864. He wasted little time after his arrival, and soon he had built a house, bought some cattle, and added a corral and slaughterhouse.

After a Fort Douglas commander claimed that Popper's land was property of the U.S. Army and ordered the rancher to move out, Popper gathered all of his funds and took his case to higher powers. Eventually, the government relented and granted him the land in 1875; under his watch it became known as Popperton Place. He owned the property until 1907, when it was appropriated for Fort Douglas. Officers built their homesteads there, establishing the Federal Heights neighborhood.

The land was subdivided and advertised extensively in local newspapers, bragging that "$50,000 in improvements and high-class restrictions" had been lavished upon the project. Federal Heights promised "spectacular views" and "pure air, the life above the smoke." But escape from the pollution caused by coal smoke was not the only draw: From its inception, Federal Heights was billed as an upscale neighborhood of wealthy homeowners who built large, stylish homes. The ad copy worked—no longer was the area thought of as a place for slaughter yards, but as one of the most fashionable neighborhoods in the city. Popperton Place is still known as a subdivision within Federal Heights.

American suburbs in the early 20th century included amenities that fostered a comfortable, family-oriented environment. These Federal Heights homes in 1913 feature plenty of greenery and large yards.

For some, Federal Heights (seen here in 2009) is a hiker's dream: A particular advantage is the location of Federal Heights in relationship to the local canyons. The proximity provides easy availability to many trailheads that lead to wilderness areas beyond.

Central City

A CHANGE IS A-COMIN'

Located east of downtown, Central City was developed from 1870 to 1946 as Salt Lake City shifted from an agricultural community to that of an industrial and commercial society. Working-class families replaced farmers, and as more non-Mormons moved into the area, Salt Lake City transitioned from an insular pioneer religious community to a larger, more mainstream city like those found throughout the West.

One of the oldest residential areas existing in Salt Lake City, the original ten-acre blocks in Central City (which run from 700 East to State Street and from 1300 South to South Temple) remain intact today, although the original agricultural area was divided into smaller, denser lots as early as the 1860s. Platted and distributed to the settlers using a lottery system, each lot was supposed to have a house located in the center with fruit trees, and chickens, a horse, and a cow in the backyard.

A VARIETY OF HOMES

At the turn of the 19th century, this section of the city was attractive to the middle- and lower-working class because of the modestly priced houses, accessibility to downtown jobs, and proximity to easy public transportation—streetcar lines connected neighborhoods throughout the city with the downtown business district. Affordable housing was constructed to provide homes for the masses

of laborers, tradespeople, and clerks who worked in the new industrial enterprises. Streets of modest t-cottages, bungalows, and eventually FHA houses (houses built with FHA-approved standards and a simple floor plan that included only the rooms that a family needed) popped up throughout Central City.

As workers moved on to other cities, or moved south to the suburbs, the neighborhood's population continued to fluctuate, and for a time it was quite unstable. However, the waxing and waning of the population also introduced greater cultural, religious, and economic diversity. Rental housing and multi-family units were constructed to support the transient nature of the community during this time. Much of the Central City district features courts or alleys that provide access to the interior of the neighborhood's large blocks, creating more intimate domestic streetscapes. Single-family bungalow courts were

Open to the public since 1938 (around when this photo was taken), Tracy Aviary occupies eight acres of Liberty Park. Salt Lake City banker Russell Lord Tracy founded Tracy Aviary when he donated his private bird collection to the city.

Left: Riding the Ferris wheel or filling up on cotton candy at the little amusement park in Liberty Park gives visitors a taste of good old-fashioned fun. The park is seen here in 2009.

developed in the center of some of Central City's blocks: Hawkes Court features eclectic Victorian housing built between 1898 and 1911, and Hawthorne Avenue is a small interior street of 800-square-foot bungalows.

But Central City wasn't all affordable working-class housing—it certainly had a ritzy district. The neighborhood's north end, which served as an extension of the larger mansions found on South Temple, was an exception to the more modest housing found in the southern part of the district. Examples of the sort of high-style architecture found in this section of the city include the Queen Anne–style mansion that former City Mayor Francis Armstrong had built for his wife in 1893 (that now serves as the Armstrong Mansion Bed and Breakfast); the 1898 O. J. Salisbury house designed by Frederick Hale, which has been converted into a funeral home; and the Bamberger Mansion, built for Governor Simon Bamberger, who was elected in 1916 and bridged the gap between non-Mormons and Mormons.

YOUR NEIGHBORHOOD STORE

Small single- or two-story commercial blocks are still sporadically found throughout the area, offering dry goods or fresh farm products for sale. In the city's early days, many of the commercial buildings were small-scale structures attached to single-family residential houses. Hale's Market continues to serve as a local store with a residence attached, and the historic Edward Hance House at 580 East 300 South has Art Floral attached to the front.

Perhaps the largest commercial institution in the area, Trolley Square was constructed by the Utah Light and Power Company in the early 1900s to support the growth of the transportation networks—within six years, 144 trolleys served the valley from this location. Perched high above at 700 East, the water tower historically held 50,000 gallons of water used for emergency firefighting. Trolley Square consists of a complex of mission-style trolley barns, a relatively rare sight in the city. In the 1970s, the square and its buildings were converted into a shopping center.

GREEN SPACE

Landscaping was an important part of the development of Salt Lake City, and the city designers included grass medians and uniform setbacks and tree planting. In line with the City Beautiful movement of the early 20th century, the median running down the center of 600 East toward South Temple extended the green space, creating a boulevard running through Central City. These grass medians can be found on several north-south streets; their presence made the city not only lovely to look at but efficient as well. Salt Lake City also was envisioned as a "Valley of Trees," so ordinances dictated the type of trees that would be planted on the major streets: thornless honey locusts on 200 East, white ash on 800 East, and sycamores on 200 South.

In 1881, the city purchased the "Big Field," an area south of 900 South, to create Liberty Park. Spread across more than 80 acres, it was the first major public park in Salt Lake City. The area was originally home to Isaac Chase's residence and mill, both of which still remain as part of the park's features. Tracy Aviary and recreational facilities, including tennis courts, a swimming pool, and a mini fair park complete with a Ferris wheel, also reside in the park.

Today in Central City, single-family homes exist alongside duplexes and multifamily housing as well as by large and small commercial spaces. The importance city planners placed on green space and street landscaping balances the emergence of shopping malls and parking lots. With its variety of residences, Central City continues to offer an affordable place to live.

Top left: Gilgal Sculpture Garden, tucked away mid-block between residences and businesses, is open daily for visitors to enjoy the imaginative sculptures of Thomas Battersby Child Jr.

Funeral streetcars were sometimes used to carry the casket and accompanying mourners to the cemetery. This Utah Light and Railway trolley, seen here in 1914, is parked at Trolley Square with the sign "Special" in the window to avoid any commuters jumping aboard.

ST. MARK'S CATHEDRAL

Daniel Tuttle was the first bishop of the Protestant Episcopal Church in Utah, a colorful character who challenged the staid history of the pioneer era. When Tuttle arrived in town on July 2, 1867, he came riding atop a stagecoach, accompanying the driver for the adventure, a rifle balancing precariously across his lap, his face streaked with dust, and his clothes more typical of an outdoorsman than a religious official.

Before the Episcopal Church laid the cornerstone for St. Mark's Cathedral in 1870, members met in Independence Hall, an ecumenical structure used by various non-Mormon congregations. It would be three years after services were first held in St. Mark's that it was officially consecrated as a cathedral. Famed glass-makers Louis Comfort Tiffany and Charles Connick designed some of the cathedral's stained glass windows in the early 20th century.

The Episcopal Church has always had a great impact on social service contributions in Utah. St. Mark's Episcopal School was the first non-Mormon school in Utah; this and other Episcopal schools carried the burden of public education in Utah until free public education began in 1890. Tuttle was also the driving force behind the building of Mt. Olivet Cemetery, a non-Mormon alternative to the Salt Lake City Cemetery.

Well-known national architect Richard Upjohn donated the blueprints for the cathedral. The nave facing the chancel is shown here in 1967.

St. Mark's Cathedral was the first non-Mormon church built in Salt Lake City, with the exception of the Independence Hall building. The church is shown here in 2009.

FIRST UNITED METHODIST CHURCH

Although renowned fur trapper and explorer (and Methodist) Jedediah Smith was the first white man to cross the Utah Territory in the 1820s, acceptance of other beliefs in the predominately Mormon community were long in coming. In 1868, Brigham Young invited Reverend A. N. Fisher to preach the first Methodist sermon in the Mormon Tabernacle. Soon after, Methodist church leaders recognized the need for a Utah mission, and they sent Reverend Hartsough to Salt Lake City. There he met with Bishop Daniel Tuttle of the Episcopal Church, who offered to share his meeting room space for Methodist services. In 1871, the original Methodist Church was built at 33 East Third South. The current building, located at 203 South 200 East, was designed by Salt Lake architect Frederick A. Hale in 1905. Members met in the Y.M.C.A. while the new building was being constructed.

In 1939, the First Methodist Episcopal Church dropped "Episcopal" from its official denominational name and became the First Methodist Church. In 1968, the name changed once again when the Methodist Church united with the Evangelical United Brethren. Today it is known as the First United Methodist Church.

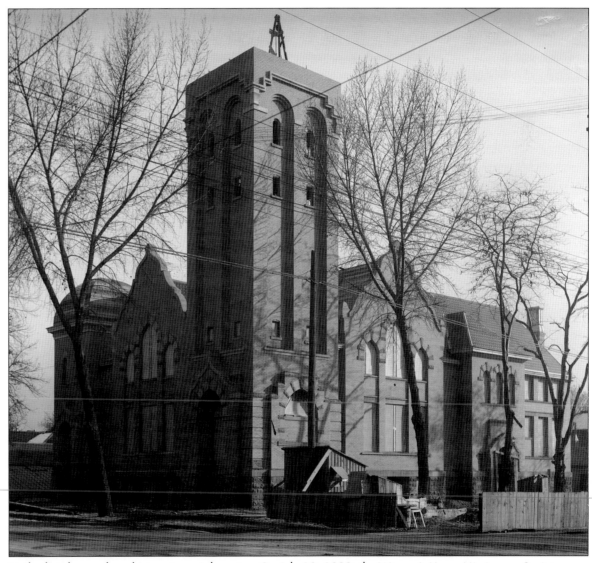

Methodists have a long history in social service. On July 10, 1880, the Women's Home Missionary Society was founded. The group was known to fight against polygamy, but Methodists made a huge, if not their greatest, contribution to Utah's education system by establishing schools and providing teachers and nurses. The church is seen here in December 1905.

FIRST UNITED METHODIST CHURCH TODAY

Since its inception, the First United Methodist Church has fostered a strong commitment to the disenfranchised and the poor, sharing its space with a wide range of social organizations, including the Tongan United Methodist Church, which holds services there in native Tongan. Since 2005, the Utah Health and Human Rights Project, a nonprofit group that serves the unique needs of refugee populations, has met in a space provided by the First United Methodist Church. More broadly, the church's work extends to locals living in poverty as well as an outreach project in Guatemala. Shown below right is the church as seen today; in the middle, the glass dome provides the interior of the church with a warm glow.

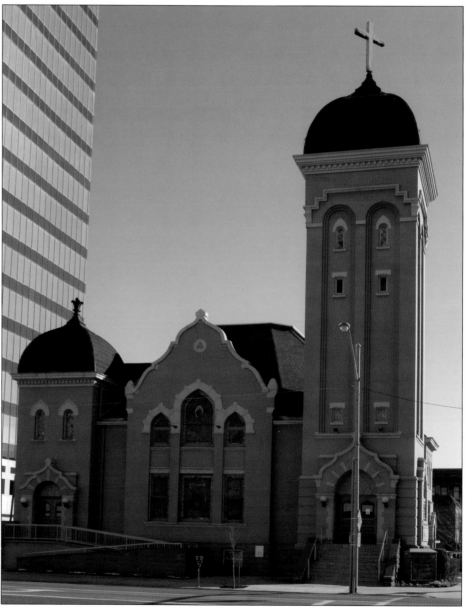

The first African Americans in Salt Lake City came with the first wave of pioneers in 1847. Trinity African Methodist Episcopal Church is shown above in the mid-20th century.

The church's detailed stained glass windows lend vibrant color to this place of worship.

TRINITY AFRICAN METHODIST EPISCOPAL CHURCH

Utah's first African American congregation was originally organized in the 1890s, but they lacked the funds to build their own church and met in homes or rented rooms. In 1907, Mary Bright, an African American cook who made a fortune cooking for miners in Leadville, Colorado, donated funds to purchase a lot for the Trinity African Methodist Episcopal (A.M.E.) Church. Two years later, their building at 239 East 600 South, designed by member Hurley Howell, was completed.

The modest brick church features Gothic revival–style influences familiar to traditional Protestant architecture. The Trinity A.M.E. Church underwent a renovation in 1976. Although the building is not particularly distinctive in terms of style, it is important as a symbol of the African American community and its social, educational, and religious activity in Utah. The church provided refuge and strength in an environment dominated by a single religious group and a particular racial and ethnic homogeneity.

Under Reverend D. D. Wilson, restoration work to the building began in 1976. Today the church appears much as it did when it was first built.

Students pose for a photo on the front steps of Oquirrh School in 1905.

OQUIRRH SCHOOL

In territorial-era Utah, small public schools located throughout the valley were typically one-room schoolhouses that served the needs of students of all ages. This gave way to consolidated schools, which combined these far-flung schools into a central school with classes for each of the separate grades. Located at 350 South and 400 East, Oquirrh School is the lone survivor of the consolidated schools built at the turn of the century. The school was designed by the esteemed architect of the State Capitol building, Richard K. A. Kletting, who created at least ten schools between 1892 and 1912.

Oquirrh School is typical of the consolidated school built during the late 19th century: classrooms located on each of the three levels were found in the four corners around a central hallway and circulation space. Its exterior combines the heavy rusticated

arches so typical of the Romanesque style with the formality and symmetry of the second renaissance revival. Upon its grand opening on September 10, 1894, *The Daily Tribune* hailed it as "the handsomest yet erected under the Board of Education. . . . [The Board] is as proud of the building as a boy is of his first pair of boots."

The growth of the city during the 1950s and '60s, and the spread of its citizens to suburbs, led to a decline in attendance at Oquirrh School. Though other turn-of-the-century schools were being razed, Oquirrh was simply closed and resold in 1973 to be used as an office complex. In 2009, the Oquirrh School building assumed its original use as the new home for the Children's Center, a nonprofit organization providing mental-health care for children.

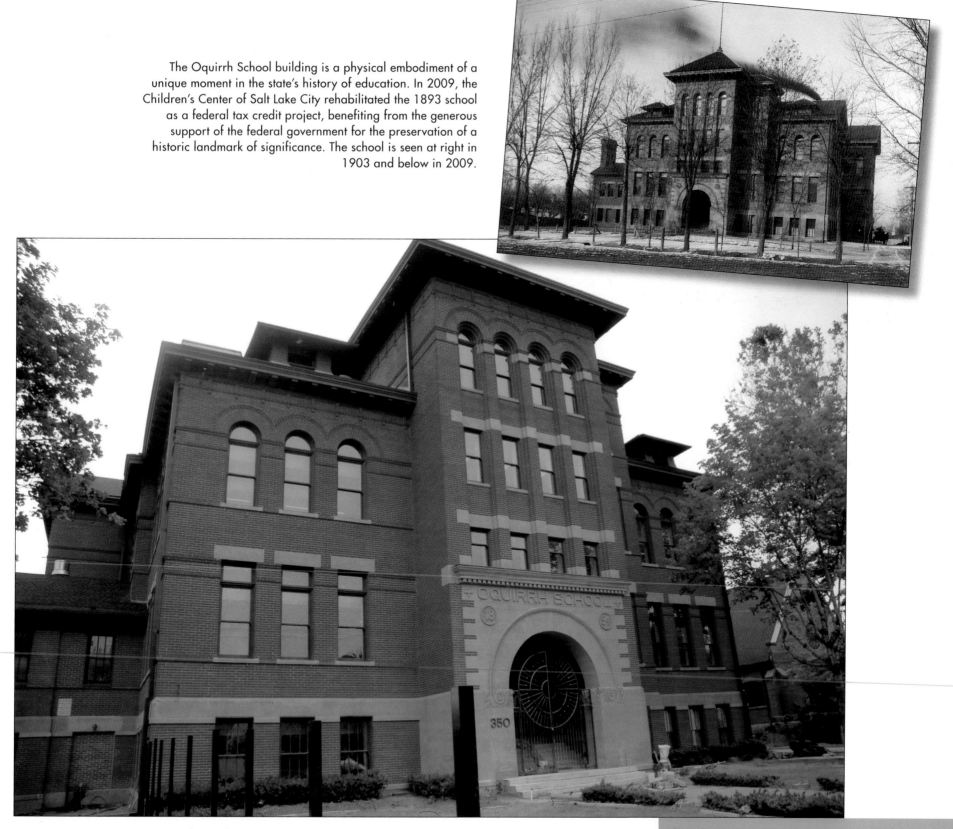

The Oquirrh School building is a physical embodiment of a unique moment in the state's history of education. In 2009, the Children's Center of Salt Lake City rehabilitated the 1893 school as a federal tax credit project, benefiting from the generous support of the federal government for the preservation of a historic landmark of significance. The school is seen at right in 1903 and below in 2009.

Jewish immigrants held services as early as the 1860s in Salt Lake City. When the cornerstone was laid for the B'nai Israel Temple (seen here in an undated photo), *The Salt Lake Tribune* described it as a "facsimile in miniature of the Great Temple in Berlin, Germany."

B'NAI ISRAEL TEMPLE

For many immigrants, the American West seemed a blank slate, a wide-open space that would provide relief from the religious and racial persecution they experienced in so many other places. Much like the Mormon pioneers, several of the early Jewish settlers who moved to Salt Lake City had been forced out of their homes. Moreover, many Jewish merchants saw the potential for economic benefit with the development of mining and the presence of the U.S. Army that came here in the 1850s and the 1860s. In 1853, Julius Gerson Brooks and his wife, Fanny, became the first permanent Jewish family to settle in the area, running a millinery shop and bakery.

B'nai Israel means "children of Israel" in Hebrew. In 1881, the B'nai Israel Congregation incorporated and built its synagogue in 1883 on 100 West and 300 South. The congregation quickly outgrew this building, however, and in 1891 a new synagogue was dedicated at 249 South 400 East. Philip Meyer, a German native, and Henry Monheim, a local architect, designed the temple. Built with kyune sandstone, the cornerstone was laid on the northwest corner of the lot, as is Jewish custom. Stained glass windows and a sweeping interior space created an environment that was elegant, extravagant, and impressive.

There was an eventual division in the congregation, and a more conservative, orthodox group called the Congregation Montefiore split off in 1899. The two groups later reunited into the Congregation Kol Ami in 1976. The B'nai Israel building is now used for private businesses.

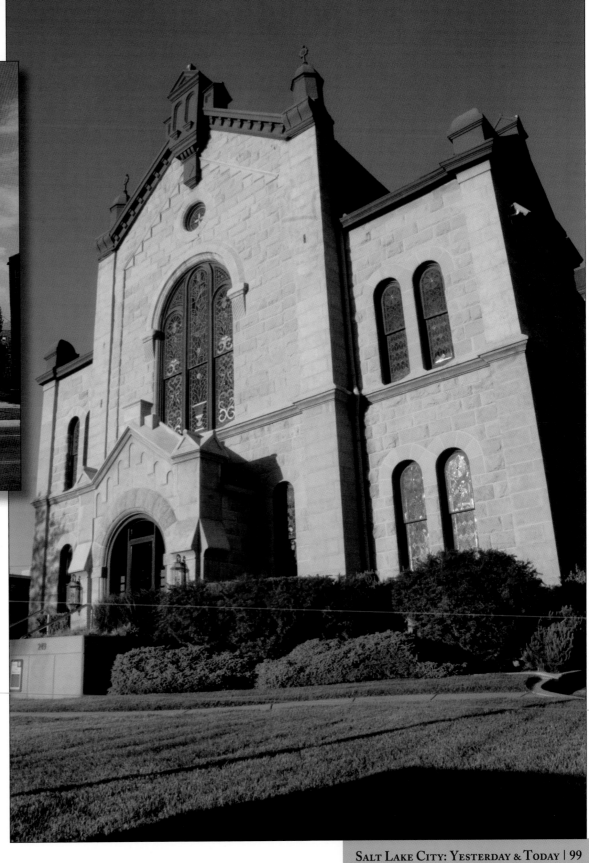

Although the Jewish population has always been relatively small in Salt Lake City, several influential Jewish merchants and businesspeople set up shop here. Samuel H. Auerbach, Simon Bamberger, the Walker Brothers, and Samuel Kahn are just a few who fought to survive in the Mormon-dominated business sector and strived to maintain their traditional religious way of life. The B'nai Israel Temple is shown above in 1910 and at right in 2009.

STREETCAR SUBURBS

In 1872, Mormon Church leaders organized the first streetcar system. After streetcars changed from mule-drawn carts to an electrified system, there were 15 miles of lines extending east and west from downtown. In the late 1880s, spurred by the growing convenience provided by the development of public transportation systems, several residential areas developed at the outskirts of the commercial core of the city. With public transportation, people were able to easily commute between their homes and their jobs in the commercial or industrial part of town. However, this deviated from what the Mormon city plan encouraged—to live in a central village and commute to farms on the edge of the city.

By 1925, a streetcar suburb called East Liberty Park was home to working- and middle-class people in modest, single-family dwellings. Another, the Waterloo suburb, was originally the location for the Wilford Woodruff farm, whose farmhouse was one of the first built in the Big Field (at the time, outside of city limits).

Non-Mormon contractors developed the streetcar suburb Lincoln Park. Some of these new subdivisions provided areas for non-Mormons to settle, where they could avoid trying to integrate themselves into the dominant Mormon communities. Featuring greater density and smaller lot sizes, the streetcar suburbs reflected the need for convenient transportation to connect to the city's commercial life. It also provided an up-and-coming glimpse at the landscape of the American dream—the single-family detached home.

Young children wait in line to check out a book or purchase a nickel candy at the Waterloo Drug Public Library Branch in 1921. The Waterloo streetcar provided easy access for residents in the area.

The Waterloo Ward Mormon Chapel, seen here circa 1910, exhibits the architectural eclecticism so popular in Utah during the late 19th century. For the Latter-day Saints in the neighborhood, this building was the center of their religious world and the heart of their social network.

Right: The 9th and 9th district has long been supported by the small commercial node found on 900 South to both the east and west.
Below: Coffee shops, restaurants, the Tower Theater, and specialty shops, such as the Blue Cockatoo Gallery, keep the local aspect of the neighborhood alive and make this area a delight to visit.

LIBERTY PARK

Like Central Park in New York City, Liberty Park at 1100 South 600 East provides a lush open space in a densely populated part of Salt Lake City and a respite from the hustle and noise of city life. The original owner of the land, Isaac Chase, received this allocation in the original "Big Field Survey" distribution of 1847. Brigham Young bought the property from Chase in 1860, planting many varieties of trees on the site. During these pioneer days, the land was also locally known as Forest Park, the Locust Patch, and Mill Farm. After Young's death in 1881, the city purchased the land for $27,500.

Also like Central Park, Liberty Park includes a combination of wild features and formal pathways. Besides the picnic pavilions, a lake, and bandstand, the park added an amusement park, tennis courts, and a swimming pool. The Tracy Aviary was built here in 1938. The park was also the home of the city zoo, until it was moved and renamed Hogle Zoo in 1931.

Today, visitors can take part in the many activities that Liberty Park—Utah's second largest urban park—has to offer. Grownups and children alike can enjoy ponds, running paths, a children's amusement park, and even the old Chase Home Museum, which is now the home of the Utah Folk Arts program.

People enjoy a leisurely canoe ride in Liberty Park in 1910. Fully in line with the Progressive Era's belief that parks contributed to the moral reform of a city's citizenry, Liberty Park became central to Salt Lake City's effort to create "the good life."

A buggy waits outside the wooden Liberty Park Pavilion on September 16, 1912.

Virtually every Utah community had a saw or gristmill that fed off streams cascading down from the nearby mountains. The Chase Mill (seen in this undated photo) is a great example of an early industrial complex, which was originally known as the Mill Farm. The mill was in operation until the 1870s.

In this photo from August 1950, amusement park visitors enjoy exciting rides and tasty treats.

A LOCAL CELEBRITY

Perhaps the most exciting acquisition within the zoo's first decade was Princess Alice, an Asian elephant named for President Theodore Roosevelt's daughter in 1916. In this postcard from 1918, Princess Alice is shown with her new baby, Prince Utah. In 1931, Princess Alice broke loose and was found wandering down 700 East, trailing clotheslines snagged during her travels through neighborhood yards. Not surprisingly, the elephant's escape prompted discussion about moving the zoo to a new location.

A map helps visitors navigate the park's 80 acres.

In this 2009 photo, a beautiful sunset colors the pond as well as the sky above. Liberty Park functions like an oasis in the midst of an urban neighborhood.

Different water fountains found in the park keep children cooled off in the hot summer months, as seen in this recent photo. Liberty Park fulfills the ambitions of Central Park designer Frederick Law Olmsted, who said, "We want a ground to which people may easily go after their day's work is done, and where they may stroll for an hour, seeing, hearing, and feeling nothing of the bustle and jar of the streets."

ISAAC CHASE HOME AND MILL

When the Mormon pioneers arrived at the Salt Lake Valley in 1847, they confronted a vast, barren valley floor with few trees and no modern amenities. A sawmill in this raw environment meant the difference between a measure of civilization and perpetual camping. Isaac Chase's sawmill was key to the city's development. After the mill was completed, Chase built his home here in 1853. Visitors often lingered on his ample front porch and enjoyed the view of the fields beyond or listened to the pump organ the family had transported across the plains when they came to Utah Territory. The Chase family lived in the house until 1860, when they moved to a house on State Street. Isaac Chase died the following year.

THE VIRGIN OF GUADALUPE

IN MEXICO, DECEMBER 12 is the annual day of the Virgin Mary, a pilgrimage day to the Basilica of the Virgin of Guadalupe in Mexico City. Believers travel from across the country to pay homage, petition for blessings, and give thanks to this patron saint of Latin American Catholics.

Manifestations of the image of the Virgin have appeared on various places: the rusty fender of a Chevy Camaro in Texas and on the broken bough of a tree in Salt Lake City. The Salt Lake image was first spotted in May 1997 by a worker who was maintaining the branches of a tree that had been damaged by lightning at 700 South and 300 East—a dark, oval shape that bore a striking resemblance to the Madonna and child.

Within weeks after the sighting, candles, photographs, and an assortment of personal items were left at the base of the tree—a testament to the power of this symbol of hope. Eventually, the city erected stairs and a platform so believers could walk to the top to gaze at the image. The likeness has since been vandalized, but the faithful still worship at the tree.

TROLLEY SQUARE

In 1906, the president of Union Pacific and Southern Pacific railroads, E. H. Harriman, purchased all streetcar lines and a controlling interest in the Utah Light and Railway Company. His progressive vision: to provide Salt Lake City with an electric trolley system, one that would prove to be one of the leading examples of such a system in the nation. He bought the most up-to-date trolley cars, and between 1908 and 1910, Harriman built a large facility of four barns to be used for storage and maintenance work. Shortly after, several apartment buildings were constructed in the area to house trolley workers and employees of nearby Troy Laundry and Salt Lake Brewing Co.

The streetcar system shut down in 1945. It would not be until 2002 that a light rail system would take again to the city streets. In the 1970s, developers converted the historic Trolley Square barn complex into specialty retail shops and restaurants. The iconic 97-foot water tower was adorned with neon lights to herald the new shopping center. Even with the high-end update, much of Trolley Square's old-fashioned charm remains intact.

Floats in parades have long been a tradition in Salt Lake City, with the Days of 47 Parade and the Utah Pride Parade competing for most popular. This 1912 float celebrates the Birth of the Fruits of Irrigation, with three women dressed in their best on the Irrigation Commission float.

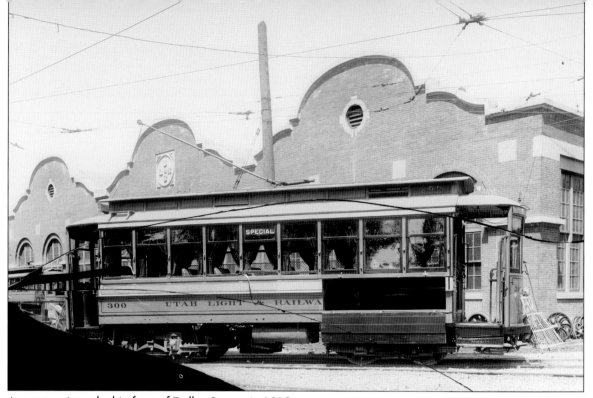

A streetcar is parked in front of Trolley Square in 1913.

One of the most distinctive landmarks in Salt Lake City is the Trolley Square Water Tower, originally designed to hold more than 50,000 gallons of water. Today, a neon sign announces that visitors have arrived at this charming shopping mall made out of an old car barn complex.

Many historic elements have found their way into the Trolley Square mall. For instance, the short bridge that links the main section of Trolley Square with the building to the north—historically the machine shop—was once a mining trestle brought to Salt Lake City from the Anaconda Mines near Tooele, Utah. In The Old Spaghetti Factory restaurant, diners can enjoy their meal inside a retired trolley car.

Thomas Battersby Child Jr. tackled the project of creating Gilgal Gardens (as seen above in 1955), with the help of Utah sculptor Maurice Brooks. Some of the stones used were as heavy as 72 tons, which Child hauled in his own truck. Believing in the power of symbol and art to capture one's religious beliefs, Child wrote, "If you want to be brought down to earth in your thinking and studying, try to make your thoughts express themselves with your hands." The word *Gilgal* literally means "circle of stones."

GILGAL SCULPTURE GARDEN

Stonemason and Mormon bishop Thomas Battersby Child Jr. imprinted his legacy in a surprising urban space, tucked away behind a couple houses on 500 South: Gilgal Sculpture Garden. Child began work on the garden when he was 57 years old; his passion and time was devoted to the Gilgal for the next 18 years until his death in 1963.

This unique garden contains 12 original sculptural arrangements, including a sphinx with the face of Joseph Smith and a larger-than-life sculpture of Child wearing brick pants. There are also more than 70 stones engraved with Mormon scriptures, philosophical sayings, and references from world literature. Child knew many people would think his garden strange. "You don't have to agree with me. You may think I am a nut, but I hope I have aroused your thinking and curiosity," he said. Eccentric and wonderfully weird, Gilgal is an otherworldly oasis amid a traditional working-class neighborhood.

The park was largely forgotten for decades save for occasional visitors and curiosity seekers. Luckily, the Friends of Gilgal Garden have raised sufficient funds to save it from destruction in the path of development and have preserved it as a Salt Lake City sculpture park.

SPHINX AND STONES

Interesting is perhaps the best word to describe the sphinx with the head of Joseph Smith (above)—a unique and unusual interpretation of religious leadership and the power of myth and symbolism all rolled into one. Smith was the original prophet, president, and leader of the Mormon movement and the person Child chose to figure most prominently in his garden of 12 sculptures, 70 engraved stones, and wooden outbuildings.

A truck loaded with hay is parked outside the 10th Ward grocery store in 1917. The store, as well as the tithing office, was the result of Brigham Young's drive for greater territorial self-sufficiency and the creation of co-ops for members to facilitate the exchange of goods.

TENTH WARD SQUARE

The early settlers laid out Salt Lake City in ten-acre blocks, which were then grouped into wards. One of the earliest was the Tenth Ward, a large, 24-block area that includes three important structures: the meetinghouse, the chapel, and the school. Today the Tenth Ward Square provides a glimpse into what life was like for 19th-century members of the LDS church.

The earliest building on the site, built in 1849, was made of adobe bricks, and it was used for both religious services and school. In 1853, this structure was replaced with a two-story adobe building, the largest ward building at the time. A Greek revival–style brick meetinghouse was built in 1873; today it is the oldest of the remaining buildings on the block. A two-story vestry with a basement was added to the west end in 1890. Today this section of the building is used as a recreation hall.

In 1909, the earlier chapel was replaced with the current Gothic revival–style chapel, but it kept some of the elements of the old building, including beautiful stained glass and a lintel that reads, "Education forms the mind, but the soul makes the man."

A district schoolhouse was built on the corner of the lot in 1887. When ward school districts were consolidated in 1890, the building was used for ward classrooms. Designed by architect Richard K. A. Kletting, the building's second floor provided additional space for students. The southwest corner of the Tenth Ward was made into a park and recreation center, farmed cooperatively by ward members who built a stone fence around the ward to protect the crops. They also built a ditch to bring water down from Emigration Canyon to water crops and trees on the site.

TENTH WARD TIMES

The upper rooms of this two-story adobe building were used for plays, and nationally known actress Maude Adams was known to have performed there. The building is also the home of the first ward band in the city, The Tenth Ward Brass Band, which began in 1868. Church, school, and entertainment were all found in the same block. This photo shows the building and street around the turn of the 19th century.

Today the Tenth Ward complex hints at what life was like years ago. Goods were purchased from small local shops such as the general store—there was no "one-stop shopping." The modern "Buy Local First" movement inspires residents to buy from small merchants rather than large corporate chain stores, returning to the 19th-century model set at the Tenth Ward Square.

Sugar House and the South End

HOW SWEET IT IS

Soon after the Mormon settlers arrived in the valley in 1847, they established Sugar House south of the city. Little physical evidence remains of the early history of Sugar House; for instance, what is now Sugar House Park and Highland High School is where Utah's first state penitentiary was located. The large farms that were owned by LDS church officials are now grassy subdivisions. Even LDS Church President Brigham Young's Forest Lawn Farmhouse was relocated from Sugar House in 1975 to This Is the Place Heritage Park in Emigration Canyon. Old manufacturing and retail centers are long gone. Despite this ebb and flow of local landmarks, Sugar House maintains a distinct identity as one of Salt Lake City's oldest and more desirable neighborhoods.

When the settlers arrived, they sectioned off a parcel of land for use as self-sufficient family farmland, which they simply called the "Big Field." In 1853, part of the Big Field (from 700 East to 2000 East and from 1300 South to 2700 South) became known as Sugar House. The name was inspired by the excitement over a sugar beet factory that was built in 1853. The presence of nearby Parley's Creek allowed for a ready source of water, which made Sugar House an important early center of industry, including mills, factories, and foundries.

Ultimately, the sugar beet mill never produced a single grain of sugar (rather, it made molasses). But obstinately, the name stuck. Over the years, the forsaken sugar mill served as a paper mill, coal yard, and railroad roundhouse. In 1928, the old mill was demolished and the historic Sugar House Monument was erected in its place at the corner of 2100 South and 1100 East.

YOUR LOCAL STORE
The historic core of Sugar House is characterized by its particular scale—that of a small commercial center. The neighborhood's planners limited the stores to only one to two stories high, and they were built to blend in with the rest of the neighborhood. Over the years, Sugar House's commercial district saw many "modernization" efforts. By the 1920s, none of the early commercial buildings remained.

Rockwood Furniture, seen here circa 1930, typifies the scale of early commercial buildings in the core of Sugar House.

Left: For 96 years, the Utah Penitentiary was located in what is now Sugar House Park, a use that couldn't be more different than the public amenity it is today. The prison is seen here at the turn of the century.

For decades, the corner of 1100 East and 2100 South was known as "Furniture Row" because of the three large stores that set up shop there: Rockwood Furniture, Granite Furniture, and Sterling Furniture. Unfortunately, all but one has closed their doors (Rockwood in 1999 and Granite in 2004). Only Sterling remains, which was first owned by Peter Madsen, one of the first furniture makers to come to the state. While Sugar House has proudly eschewed the "big box stores" in the past, the future of these buildings—as well as the iconic, rotating sign (known as a Roto-Sphere, or "sputnik") atop Granite Furniture—remains unknown as development pressures continue.

STREETCAR NEIGHBORHOODS

Early transportation routes offered convenient travel to the south end of the valley, and these lines fostered housing development along the way. Local residential architecture illustrates this trend; streets lined with modest-size bungalows highlight the desirability of the area for prospective homeowners looking for something sturdy and affordable.

Literally thousands of bungalows exist in Sugar House, a strong reminder of how the area grew, as well as the importance of availability of mass transit for residents. By 1927, the last year that a historic subdivision was platted, nearly every home was within walking distance of a streetcar line. The Salt Lake & Fort Douglas Railway provided a route along 1100 East from downtown to the south end of the city. There are several neighborhoods located within this area of the city, including Forest Dale, Highland Park, Westminster Heights, and Country Club Acres.

LDS leader and businessman George M. Cannon incorporated Forest Dale in 1901—it was considered a unique venture for a Mormon leader to try his hand at real-estate development. Cannon paid a streetcar company in order to secure its services to the area, but it proved to be more costly to build infrastructure and provide local services than he initially anticipated. In 1912, due to the high costs of municipal services, the town was unincorporated and annexed back to Salt Lake City. Today Forest Dale remains a popular area, particularly for those who visit the Forest Dale Golf Course.

Other areas in Sugar House are laden with their own history and character as well: Utah architect Taylor Woolley, who studied several years in Frank Lloyd Wright's studio in Oak Park, Illinois, designed homes in the Highland Park neighborhood. Westminster Heights arose near the Westminster College campus. Country Club Acres was developed in 1924 as an exclusive neighborhood in a rural landscape. Huge lots with large setbacks characterize the neighborhood. The Great Depression stalled the construction of several homes

Bungalow neighborhoods lined with trees are abundant in Sugar House, creating urban corridors shared by neighbors and contributing to the enormous appeal of this part of the city.

until the 1940s and '50s; however, this neighborhood maintains the exclusivity that the original local developers, the Ashton-Jenkins Company, envisioned.

DECLINE AND RENEWAL

In the early 1960s, the Interstate 80 freeway was constructed, which cut off a portion of the south end of the city. New construction of multi-family units occurred during this time, but Sugar House neighborhoods along the major transportation corridors saw an urban decline through the early '80s. A revitalization came later in the decade; this renewal, combined with the special services and spaces that mark Sugar House, have helped the area to become one of the more desirable places to live in Salt Lake City once again.

In 1947, the Sugar House Merchants worked together to clean the Sugar House Monument to celebrate the 100th anniversary of the Mormon settlers entering the valley. Today the merchants group continues to lead the community in improvement efforts, including hosting the annual Fourth of July Sugar House Arts Festival. The monument is shown below in 2009.

The curving cobblestone base of this California-style bungalow adds charm and distinction to what is otherwise a fairly straightforward house.

WESTMINSTER HEIGHTS

During the first decades of the 20th century, bungalow neighborhoods added to the architectural diversity of the city. They were also built with greater density in urban subdivisions. Unlike earlier generations of pioneer-era houses that featured the broad side of the building facing the street, the short end of the bungalow's rectangle faced the street and was dominated by an ample front porch, the style's most distinctive feature.

Because of its economic boom in the late 19th century, Salt Lake City was considered prime real estate. In the early 1900s, California developers Clark and Earl Dunshee invested in

about 50 acres of land just east of Westminster College, subdividing it within months in anticipation of the extension of the trolley line past 900 South and 1300 East.

Unfortunately, the line never materialized. The section needed a new spin: Marketing the American dream of home ownership, Westminster Heights was viewed as part of a particular upper- and middle-class, modern way of life in a location that provided expansive views of the valley. Today it is known for its beautifully detailed bungalows that reflect the sensibility of the arts and crafts style.

For families who favored the bungalow style, the front porch was the most public place in the house, announcing a tangible welcome to friends and neighbors. Interior spaces in a bungalow (such as this one circa late 1930s) moved from the most public—the living room located at the front of the house—to the dining room, kitchen, and bedrooms toward the back. The number in the foreground of the photo is an indicator used for city tax purposes.

ROBERT H. FOSTER HALL, MEN'S DORMITORY,
WESTMINSTER COLLEGE, SALT LAKE CITY, UTAH

Finished in 1926, Foster Hall was once called the "Cracker Box." After a renovation, Foster Hall was rededicated in 1994 as part of the Jewett Center for the Arts and Humanities. The building is pictured in this mid-20th century postcard.

WESTMINSTER COLLEGE

Founded in 1875, the Salt Lake Collegiate Institute opened as a prep school under the First Presbyterian Church. In 1897, the school began offering college classes as Sheldon Jackson College, named after the primary benefactor of the school. Finally, in 1902, the school was renamed Westminster College—the first accredited junior college in the intermountain area. The campus also moved from its previous downtown location to 1300 East and 1700 South in the Sugar House neighborhood in 1911.

The Westminster campus is recognized for its beautiful landscaping as well as its architecture. Notable buildings on campus include Converse Hall, the first building at Westminster College and a historic center-piece that is often named as the most recognizable entrance into the school; Foster Hall, built in 1917 originally as a men's dorm; and Payne Gymnasium, designed by local architect Walter E. Ware.

In 2008, Westminster was named one of "The 366 Best Colleges" in the country according to the Princeton Review's annual guide.

Westminster College has undergone a significant period of growth during the past decade and a half. New buildings have been added to its repertoire, including the Giovale Library, the Jewitt Center for the Performing Arts, and the Emma Eccles Jones Conservatory. Renovations have brought older buildings into a new generation of use, including Bamberger and Converse halls (seen here in 2009).

Impressive, high-styled buildings such as the old Ferry Hall (seen here on the right in 1918) were built to relay a sense of grandeur. But more importantly, these buildings were the backdrop to the education of young people. Here they were introduced to a liberal education and charged to go out into the world to serve and engage in a lifetime of learning.

SUGAR HOUSE MONUMENT

One of the neighborhood's most recognizable identifiers, the Sugar House Monument stands centrally located at 1100 East and 2100 South, just west of Sugar House Park. Built by Millard Fillmore Milan, the monument reflects the cohesiveness of the merchants in the area. The monument was built in 1930 in the tradition of ancient vertical obelisks, with its 50-foot-high art deco shaft situated on a plaza in the main intersection of Sugar House. The monument features angular decorative patterns on its sides, and the carved limestone band on its bottom shows the state flower, the sego lily, amid the sun, the stars, the planets, and a crescent moon. Two eight-foot-tall bronze figures sit at the base of the monument.

Despite the local sugar mill's failure, the structure was built to honor the history of the sugar beet industry in Utah. The plaque on the north side of the structure reads, "Erected in recognition of the first effort made to manufacture beet sugar in western America."

The monument has seen the many evolutions of the neighborhood over the years, but it has remained the constant. The city has shown its commitment to this local landmark with restoration and cleaning of the monument.

There are two massive bronze figures at the base of the Sugar House Monument (seen here in this mid-20th century photo). One was inspired by a local worker the sculptor had seen carrying stones to the construction site. The female figure was modeled after Marjorie Lewis, a friend of the sculptor, to represent the richness and abundance found in the Salt Lake Valley.

SHOPPING IN SUGAR HOUSE

The corner of 2100 South and 1100 East has always been the central intersection of Sugar House. Although it has changed dramatically, the area continues to be the heart of the commercial district. *Top left:* From the start, commercial buildings were designed on a scale that would blend into the surrounding residential neighborhoods. Granite Furniture is seen here in the 1930s. *Top right:* Although Granite Furniture is now closed, its rotating Roto-Sphere is still a local icon. *Bottom right:* The Commons at Sugar House was built in 1998 and is home to bigger chain stores, while across and down the street, local businesses continue to serve the community. The area is seen here in 2009.

The Wasatch Mountains, seen here in recent times, offer an exquisite backdrop to Sugar House Park. Jogging trails, picnic areas, and playgrounds are found along the gracefully looping road that winds its way around the perimeter and through the center of the park.

SUGAR HOUSE PARK/FORMER UTAH PENITENTIARY

It's a good bet that most joggers, bicyclists, and picnickers who enjoy Sugar House Park do not realize that the site was once the location of Utah's first territorial prison. Built in 1855 on ten acres, the prison complex was eventually expanded to 120 acres. Prisoners were put to work in the fields growing fresh food for use in their kitchen. But the prison certainly had some structural problems: It was surrounded by a 12-foot-high and four-foot-thick adobe wall, which broke down into mud when wet. Needless to say, the wall was not very effective at keeping prisoners inside the prison; over the years, about a quarter of the cons escaped.

After the prison closed in 1951, it was dictated that the prison site (minus the acreage on which Highland High School now stands) "be used perpetually for public purposes." A nonprofit organization was created in 1957 to manage the park and continues to manage it today. Every day, Sugar House Park attracts plenty of visitors who come to enjoy the park's many features: a central pond, as well as several picnic areas, playgrounds, open grassy areas, soccer and softball fields, basketball courts (including a large one donated by the Utah Jazz), and a trail around its perimeter. In winter, happy sledders zip down the park's large, snow-covered hills.

LOCKED UP IN SUGAR HOUSE

Above left: The prisoners' quarters are pictured here in 1875; *above right:* a postcard shows the prison circa 1905. The Utah Penitentiary represents the presence of the rule of law—even the Mormon leaders had to conform to the restrictions put in place by the U.S. Congress and Utah Territory. *Bottom left:* A series of photos taken in the 1880s (such as this one from 1886) during the Underground period, when federal marshals chased polygamists throughout the region, depict groups of serious patriarchs posing in the prison yard, religious martyrs of a sort, imprisoned for their practices. It is a unique moment in Utah history, captured by the impressive spaces of the penitentiary— land that would later become a much beloved community park.

THE SPRAGUE LIBRARY

As one of the few remaining historic properties in the heart of Sugar House, the Sprague Library is a sentimental favorite. The library, named in honor of Joanna Sprague, opened in November 1914, and it continues to represent a national dedication to the concept of literacy as the common currency of democratic government. For more than 90 years, the library has provided locals with book discussion groups, public lectures, and a range of books from classical literature to the most current popular novels. In 1935, the American Library Association designated the Sprague Library as the "Most Beautiful Branch Library in America," recognizing the library's importance at the heart of the city, and its role in creating an educated citizenry.

Beginning in 1989–90, the Salt Lake County Library system restored the building in a series of moves to adapt the original library space for contemporary use. In April 2001, an important addition was added to the back: a landscaped plaza connecting the library to the Sugar House Commons development. The construction also increased the total square footage to 200,000 feet. In the past, sturdy card catalogues were used to organize the collection, but today computers are a mainstay. The Sprague Library has successfully been ushered into the 21st century for a new generation of avid readers to enjoy.

Joanna Sprague, head librarian for the Salt Lake Public Library between 1903 and 1940, was responsible for much of the planning for the Sugar House branch (pictured here in 1929). The plans were ambitious, driven by the desire to acknowledge the area's natural and social contexts. She said, "It was felt that the exterior should fit the park surroundings and not be of the usual and conventional type."

A group of schoolchildren read in the Sprague Library in 1916.

A nod to the neighborhood's unique history, a sculpture of a giant sugar beet sits outside the current Sprague Library (seen at left and below in 2009). Boasting large, airy rooms and plenty to read, the branch remains a local favorite.

FOREST DALE

As the 20th century grew near, the Sugar House section known as Forest Dale grew rapidly, and young people especially "flocked to this part of the city." Brigham Young originally owned the land. Although Young never actually lived there (one of his wives did), he named the land Forest Farm because of the grove of walnut and fruit trees that grew near Fairmont Spring, which made the area well suited for farming. In 1889, the land was bought, developed, and renamed by LDS leader and businessman George M. Cannon. "Forest Dale" was briefly incorporated as its own city but unincorporated when it proved too difficult and expensive to provide municipal services to its residents.

Forest Dale was home to the oldest golf course in Utah, the Salt Lake Country Club. Built in 1905, the Mission-style clubhouse was built by local architect and golf enthusiast Frederick A. Hale. In the 1920s, the ever-expanding green—now known as the Forest Dale Golf Course—moved east to its current location at 2375 South 900 East, where it continues to offer hours of entertainment for duffers of all skill levels. The clubhouse has been added to the Utah Historic Register.

The nine-hole Forest Dale Golf Course was purchased by Salt Lake City in 1935. This municipal course is friendly to new golfers and pros alike.

Above: Men tee off near the clubhouse at the Salt Lake Country Club in 1910. When the Salt Lake Country Club built the Forest Dale clubhouse in 1905, it was the first clubhouse built specifically for golf in the state. *Right:* The Country Club pavilion is shown here in 1909.

LIVING AND LEARNING

From the first, Salt Lake City was an orderly city, featuring a strong orthogonal (or right-angled) orientation and alignment with the two dominant mountain ranges, forming a legible edge on both sides of the valley. Within a decade after the Mormon settlers arrived in the Salt Lake Valley in 1847, city blocks stretched to the east and west; by 1867, the regular ten-acre-block pattern extended to 1300 East and 900 South. Houses dotted the East Bench as early as the 1860s. But water (or lack thereof) proved to be as big an obstacle for the East Bench neighborhoods as it had been for the Avenues when it was first settled in the 1850s.

FORT DOUGLAS

Access to clean water was often a problem for the growing city, but when Fort Douglas diverted water out of Red Butte Canyon for the federal troops stationed there after 1862, the city supply was cut even further. Always critical to the location of settlements along the Wasatch Front, proximity to water could make or break a town—or neighborhoods that fought over scarce resources.

The Third California Volunteer Infantry came to the Utah Territory in 1862. Originally, their charge was to protect the Overland Trail mail lines that stretched through the valley toward the East Coast. The infantry were also in the region to monitor the moves of The Church of Jesus Christ of Latter-day Saints. Led by Colonel Patrick E. Connor, troops laid the foundation for Fort Douglas, which was named by President Abraham Lincoln for the deceased Illinois Senator Stephen A. Douglas. Although the first buildings were crude log structures and adobe buildings, before long the fort was laid out according to the cardinal points of the compass and oriented around a central parade ground, now known as Stilwell Field. While Fort Douglas is still at the site, much of it has changed: More than a century later, Stilwell Field is now a part of the University of Utah and is used for events such as concerts and lacrosse games. In 1975, Fort Douglas was named a National Historic Landmark.

EAST BENCH LIVING

New theme neighborhoods popped up on the East Bench after the turn of the

It is hard to imagine how bleak the landscape appeared in 1862 when Connor's troops came to Utah Territory. The area that is now Fort Douglas (as seen above) was virtually devoid of trees.

Left: This field of red and white—the University of Utah's colors—implies unity, a love of tradition, and pride in the school's football team.

century, offering white-collar, middle-class family homes with styles mirroring national trends. The Harvard/Yale and Normandie Heights subdivisions feature period revival homes, ranging in size from modest cottages measuring less than 1,500 square feet to grand homes larger than 5,000 square feet. Red and brown brick Tudor revival-style homes often featured characteristic turrets, beveled panes and stained glass windows, and cast-iron metal work that created a picturesque landscape of taste, elegance, and formality.

Bungalow neighborhoods, such as Westmoreland Place on 1500 East and 1300 South, built in the 1910s, featured Craftsman-style homes taken from pattern books popularized in Southern California. These houses, with sweeping eaves, cobblestone columns, and distinc- tive front porches all on narrow, tree-lined streets, created a distinctive environment perfect for family life. The accessibility to the city's commercial district made it attractive as well. Street car lines running up 900 and 1300 South and along 900 and 1100 East made it easy for businesspeople to live on the edges of town and work in the down-town district. Eventually the automobile connected the East Bench with the city,

The first decade at the new East Bench campus of the University of Utah was one of significant growth. Here surveyors and workers struggle in a field with bushes that reach as high as their waists in 1907. Today this rough field is a formal garden with paths, trees, and streets—the future location of the Park Building.

establishing a more distinct pattern of residential living separate from where one worked.

UPPER EDUCATION AND BEYOND

With vehicles driving to and from campus, next to downtown Salt Lake City, the University of Utah is the second-greatest traffic generator in the Salt Lake Valley. Stretching from University Street (or 1400 East) to the west and the foothills of the Wasatch Mountains to the east, and from 100 South and 500 South, the institution is the state's flagship research university, recognized throughout the country for the strength of its professional schools, hospital complex, and distinctive programs.

When the University of Utah was founded on February 28, 1850, it was noted as the first state university west of the Mississippi River—a major coup for a burgeoning community. Originally named the University of Deseret, classes were first held in two private homes for only male students. In 1851, classes were moved to the 13th Ward School House. In 1892, the school's name was changed to the University of Utah.

The histories of the University of Utah and Fort Douglas have been intertwined since 1894, when Congress granted a 60-acre tract of land from the Fort Douglas Military Reservation. In the late 1990s, University of Utah President Bernie Machen decided that the best "re-use" of Fort Douglas would be as a residential village for student housing.

At the same time, Salt Lake City received the bid for the 2002 Winter Olympic Games as well as federal funding to build new student housing. During the Games, 4,000 athletes, trainers, and officials stayed at the Olympic village at historic Fort Douglas.

It's hard to imagine that just 155 years prior, Brigham Young and his group of Mormon pioneers descended upon what is now known as Emigration Canyon. That same trail still exists, but now the canyon mouth south of Red Butte ends at local landmarks such as the This is the Place Heritage Park and Hogle Zoo. Today, the East Bench is a district transformed into a place of learning, fun, and family.

Every host city hopes to incorporate traditional elements as well as something new and unique into the Olympics. Pictured above is the colorful opening ceremony of the 2002 Winter Olympics, held in Rice-Eccles Stadium.

GILMER PARK

The Gilmer Park neighborhood is one of the most distinct environments in the city both architecturally and geographically. Sitting on a steeply sloped hill rising from 1100 East to 1300 East, much of Gilmer Park runs along a canyon edging Red Butte Creek. In 1888, John and Mary Gilmer built their home at the end of a curving driveway near the corner of 900 South and 1100 East. John made his wealth in a wide range of occupations, working at various times as a mining operator, government mail contractor, and partner in the Gilmer and Salisbury Overland Stage Company. A decade later, a newly organized golf club, the Salt Lake Country Club, used the Gilmer house as their clubhouse before moving to a location near Forest Dale in 1905. Seeing a unique opportunity for a subdivision on the beautiful site, Mary and her son Jay organized the Gilmer Realty Company and divided the land into marketable lots in 1909.

Architect Taylor Woolley designed the layout and landscaping plan for the neighborhood, which includes irregularly shaped blocks, winding streets, and community green spaces. Best known for the time he spent working with Frank Lloyd Wright at the turn of the century, Woolley depended on natural landscaping and retaining walls as character-defining elements. Neighborhood restrictive covenants were enacted that required buildings be made to "ensure beauty and permanence that should enhance the value of the property."

Gilmer Park is known for its vast array of architectural designs, including Tudor-, Prairie-, and Craftsman-style houses built primarily with brick, stucco, or wood. The area is also well known for its bungalows and Arts and Crafts-style homes. In these undated photos, the contrast between this modernist house (bottom) and the more traditional designs that make up the majority of Gilmer Park's homes (top) is extreme. Still, this unique glass, concrete, and wood house opens up to the natural character of the canyon in appealing ways.

IN THE GREEN

After World War I, Gilmer Park was promoted as both a beautiful place to live and an ideal location for family life. A local newspaper guaranteed, "When building a home, think first of your wife and children and of their permanent happiness. If you build in Gilmer Park, you will always have a REAL home, where you and your family will enjoy every comfort and convenience." In these recent photos, it's easy to see Gilmer Park's appeal.

EAST BENCH NEIGHBORHOODS

WESTMORELAND PLACE

In 1913, borrowing from the popularity of bungalow neighborhoods in California, Earl and Clark Dunshee bought land for an exclusive new subdivision. They called the area Westmoreland Place, located on Salt Lake City's East Bench near an anticipated streetcar line. Advertisements marketing the lots in the new subdivision described it as an ideal location en route to the new country club. Lush parks along the entrance at 1300 South and 1500 East set the standard for elegance and charm. Many of the homes in Westmoreland Place neighborhood are popular Arts and Crafts or California bungalow designs that feature natural materials, ample front porches, and distinctive wood trim, and embody a sense of the California lifestyle. Over time, period revival–style cottages mixed in with these original bungalow homes.

Reflecting the City Beautiful Movement of the turn-of-the-century reform era, Westmoreland Place landscaping evoked the pastoral life, a desirable contrast with the grit and grime of the city. In this undated photo, large lawns and landscaping illustrate the typical Westmoreland Place home.

Middle-class families moved into subdivisions in Westmoreland Place, but regardless of their financial situations—these cottages are modest in size—they wanted their homes to project a certain image. A picturesque representation of an earlier time is portrayed here in 2009 with the the half-timber and steeply pitched rooflines of the Tudor revival style.

HARVARD/YALE AND NORMANDIE HEIGHTS

Two of the most charming and intimate residential neighborhoods on Salt Lake City's East Bench are the Harvard/Yale and the adjoining Normandie Heights subdivisions. In 1913, a contractor named Samuel Campbell developed the Yalecrest and Normandie Heights subdivisions and bought land on what would be known as Princeton and Laird Avenues. Campbell eventually built more than 60 houses on these two streets.

White-collar families built most of the homes in these neighborhoods at the beginning of the 20th century. The earliest houses built were bungalows in a prairie style. Later, in the decades before the Great Depression, the Tudor and colonial revival styles were by far the most popular, giving the area the distinctive character for which it is best known. Another distinguishing feature of the neighborhood is Red Butte Creek, which flows down a ravine that cuts down the south side of Yale Avenue and creates a canyonlike backyard for many residents.

The name of this unique neighborhood connotes prestige and evokes images of the tree-lined paths of Ivy League colleges on the East Coast. Located conveniently near both the University of Utah and downtown, the district is best known for its period revival–style architecture. These neighborhood homes are shown here in 2009.

MOUNT OLIVET CEMETERY

The Salt Lake City Cemetery was the area's first graveyard, but Mount Olivet Cemetery was its second—as well as the first cemetery for non-Mormons. Episcopal Bishop Daniel S. Tuttle established the burial ground in 1874. By working together with a Fort Douglas commander, Tuttle was able to petition the U.S. Congress for 20 acres of land.

Congress also appropriated a salary for a superintendent and called for a volunteer board of directors. Some of the most powerful members of the non-Mormon communities rose to the challenge, including representatives from the Episcopal, Presbyterian, Congregational, Baptist, and Methodist churches, as well as leadership from Fort Douglas. Water rights to Red Butte and Emigration creeks were included in the original deed, which over time ensured that the cemetery would be lush and verdant even during the dry summer months. The original land eventually expanded to include 88 acres, only half of which is developed. Many of Utah's rich and powerful are buried at Mount Olivet, including Governor George H. Dern, David Keith, Thomas Kearns, and Utah's Silver Queen, Susanna Bransford Emery Holmes Delitch Engalitcheff.

Top: A gravesite is shown in Mount Olivet Cemetery in 1916.
Bottom: Before automobiles became popular, the streetcar running east on 500 South (seen here in 1909) provided easy access to Mount Olivet.

Although six lanes of traffic on 500 South separate the two, the unique view of the University of Utah from Mount Olivet (shown in 2009) is evocative of the layering of city life: The energy, activity, and vitality of the academic experience forms a counterpoint to the quiet of a landscape memorializing those who have passed.

Mount Olivet's statuary is reminiscent of that in an English Victorian cemetery, with angels, obelisks, arches, figures kneeling in prayer, and even a sculpture of a tree trunk. Its streets meander around a forestlike natural environment that creates gentle nodes and alcoves for quiet thought. This monument commemorating the life of Julie Hanson suggests the wonderful exuberance of children at play.

RICE-ECCLES STADIUM

Cummings Field is shown here in 1906. A wooden fence runs along the perimeter of the field. Uncovered wooden bleachers provide seating for enthusiastic fans.

The two sandstone-clad towers of the University of Utah's Rice-Eccles Stadium form a dramatic landmark on Salt Lake City's East Bench. From the towers, one can enjoy spectacular views of the Salt Lake Valley extending west to the Oquirrh Mountains, the Great Salt Lake, and beyond. Finished in time for the opening and concluding ceremonies of the 2002 Winter Olympic Games, the stadium also hosts University of Utah football games, and until 2008, Real Salt Lake soccer matches. Between the two towers, stadium box, suites, and club levels, the stadium comfortably seats approximately 45,000 spectators.

The outdoor venue, originally named Ute Stadium, was built in 1927. Over the years, it underwent a number of remodeling changes. In 1997, the stadium started a large, $50-million expansion in preparation for the Olympic Games. Architects recommended the stadium be replaced rather than expanded, and a new configuration of seats would form a bowl of continuous rows of seats running from the field to the top.

The remodeling of Rice-Eccles Stadium and the location of the Olympic Cauldron Plaza on the site illustrate the profound impact the Winter Games had on the University of Utah campus. Perhaps the most significant addition was the Olympic Village at Fort Douglas, where thousands of new dorm rooms, suites, and apartments built for the event are now offered as comfortable housing opportunities for university students.

Considering the high-tech helmets and padding worn by modern football teams, the gear worn by these men in 1907 is simple, even minimal, in comparison. An overhang on the east side proudly spells out "UTAH."

This aerial photograph of the Rice-Eccles Stadium was taken in the 1960s, decades before the towers and structures on the west elevation were built to accommodate the 2002 Winter Olympics. A veritable forest of trees on the south end predated the Olympic plaza, and the stadium itself provided seating for tens of thousands fewer persons than its modern equivalent.

Today the UTA light rail system conveniently delivers loyal fans clothed in red to the stadium parking lot. The light rail gives people a green alternative to driving en masse to games in vehicles from all across the valley.

Demonstrating the layering that is so much a part of the city/campus relationship, this view shows the stadium, the apartments below, and the breathtaking panorama of the Wasatch Mountain range beyond. Each are important and distinct—the city, campus, and the natural world blend in a pleasing way. The two stadium towers are important landmark features on the East Bench, marking the presence of the university in the Salt Lake Valley.

IN FEBRUARY 2002, Salt Lake City hosted the XIX Olympic Winter Games. More than 2,399 athletes and 1.5 million visitors descended upon Salt Lake City, and the whole world was watching. The games were officially opened by President George W. Bush and managed by Mitt Romney, the future governor of Massachusetts. The spectacular opening events, held in the University of Utah's Rice-Eccles Stadium, featured Grammy Award–winning artist LeAnn Rimes, who sang "Light the Fire Within," the official song and motto of the 2002 Olympic Winter Games. The Mormon Tabernacle Choir sang the "The Star-Spangled Banner," and composer John Williams's "Call of the Champions" was performed by the Choir and the Utah Symphony Orchestra.

The Olympic cauldron stands amid a row of flags from around the world.

During the opening ceremonies of the first Olympics held since the September 11, 2001, terrorist attacks, International Olympic Committee President Jacque Rogge addressed the subject: "Your nation is overcoming a horrific tragedy, a tragedy that has affected the whole world. We stand united with you in the promotion of our common ideals, and hope for world peace."

A distinctive feature of the 2002 games was the inclusion of extreme sports—snowboarding, moguls, and aerials dazzled crowds.

The women's bobsled event debuted at the games, and for the first time since 1948, the skeleton race—a high-speed sled race in which racers can accelerate up to 5Gs—returned as a medal sport. Bobsledder Vonetta Flowers became the first African American athlete to win a gold medal at the winter games. Since then, each Olympic venue has been turned into a public facility.

THE UNIVERSITY OF UTAH

When Congress established the Utah Territory in 1850, they demonstrated a strong commitment to education, tacking on a clause to the act granting $5,000 annually for support of the University of Deseret. Its first class included 25 men, but in the second year women were allowed to attend. Classes were held in private residences and also public places. Because of crop failure, however, the school lost the grant and was closed from 1853 to 1867.

The university began classes once again, but it had no permanent home. Just before his death in 1892, president John R. Park asked Congress for a grant of 60 acres of land from Fort Douglas. In 1892, the school changed its name to the University of Utah; two years later, Congress finally granted 60 acres to be used for a new campus. The state hired one of its most talented architects, Richard K. A. Kletting, to design the initial campus layout and school buildings. Today, the University of Utah boasts many modern amenities, such as the light rail track leading downtown, renovations to Rice-Eccles Stadium, and a campus hotel.

Top: World War I soldiers about to be deployed to Europe listen to words of encouragement from university administration, faculty, and civic leaders. *Bottom:* Male and female students study in the student library in the Emory Building in the late 1890s.

Before the renamed University of Utah moved to the top of 200 South and University Street, the University of Deseret was located downtown. The campus's main building was University Hall, at the location of today's West High School. This undated photo shows the back of the main hall, a playing field, and five rows of bleachers to the side.

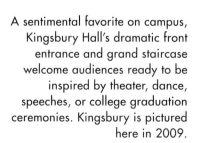

A sentimental favorite on campus, Kingsbury Hall's dramatic front entrance and grand staircase welcome audiences ready to be inspired by theater, dance, speeches, or college graduation ceremonies. Kingsbury is pictured here in 2009.

FORT DOUGLAS

Soon after the pioneers arrived in the valley, the U.S. government debated how to best intervene and establish federal rule. The Third California Volunteer Infantry arrived in Salt Lake in 1862, but the Civil War diverted much of the attention away from the goings-on of the Latter-day Saints in the Great Basin Kingdom. After the war ended, however, the flood of westward-bound migrants prompted the government to move to protect the Overland Trail, used by wagon trains moving across the Rocky Mountains, and establish more direct lines of communication between the East and the West.

The leader of the infantry, Colonel Patrick E. Connor, was given the task of establishing federal control in Utah Territory. He had Camp Douglas built along the rocky foothills of the Wasatch Mountains, particularly in Red Butte Canyon. Connor initially considered this a temporary encampment, not anticipating that the fort would still be used in the 21st century. Soon after they arrived, his soldiers built log and adobe post buildings, as well as ten Gothic revival–style cottages running along Officer's Circle, which provided housing for leaders of the various units. Six new barracks, a commanding officer's quarters, and a hospital were built in the 1870s.

The site grew in importance over time, and in 1878, Camp Douglas became Fort Douglas. During World War II, the post was used for training and mobilizing, as well as a prisoner-of-war camp. Later, Fort Douglas served as a post for U.S. Army, Marine, and Navy Reserve Units.

In this early image from 1898, soldiers struggle to move unwieldy wagons bearing cannons toward Stilwell Field at the center of the fort. A handwritten note on the back of the photo marks this as "Battery A and B Drilling at Fort Douglas."

Images such as this one remind us that the fort was simply an abstraction without the men who lived and worked there. Far from home and their families, these young soldiers sit down for a meal at the Hospital Mess Hall circa 1918.

7234. Enlisted Men's Quarters, Fort Douglas, Utah.

FORT DOUGLAS HISTORICAL PARK

Above: This postcard from the 1930s or '40s shows "The Enlisted Men's Quarters" at Fort Douglas. *Left:* Today, the Fort Douglas grounds includes the historical park (seen here in 2009) and the Fort Douglas Military Museum, which offers visitors the chance to learn about the history of the fort and see exhibits detailing American wars, weaponry, and the lives of the men and women who have lived there.

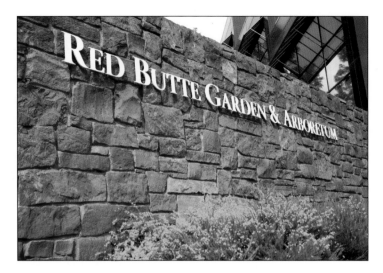

RED BUTTE GARDEN & ARBORETUM

Red Butte Canyon was important to Salt Lake City's expansion and development, as well as its architecture. Sandstone quarried at Red Butte was used for literally hundreds of local houses, public buildings, and churches throughout the valley. Today, the canyon is a popular destination for hiking, picnics, and mountain biking, offering easy access from the University of Utah and Fort Douglas.

Located at the mouth of the canyon, the Red Butte Garden & Arboretum functions as a sort of natural teaching library of the area's abundant native species of plants. In fact, learning has always been at the core of this space. Beginning in 1930, Dr. Walter P. Cottam, chairman of the Botany Department at the University of Utah, used a plot of land on campus for plant research. In 1961, state legislature designated the land as the State Arboretum. The garden opened to the public in 1985.

Through the years, Red Butte Garden has functioned like an eco-intermediary, mitigating the difference between the built spaces of Fort Douglas and the university to the west and the wildness of the canyon to the east.

As seen in the top right photo from 1929, workers quarried stone used for building dams, foundations, and countless houses in the valley below at Red Butte Canyon. Today, Red Butte Canyon (shown in the bottom photo in 2009) serves as a beautiful outdoor teaching museum, advocating xeriscaping, or the use of native and drought-tolerant plants.

CHRISTMAS STREET

A **FAVORITE LOCAL OUTING** during the holidays is driving up "Christmas Street," a yearly pilgrimage during the month of December. Although the lights at Temple Square are hard to beat for the sheer density, variety, and brilliance, Christmas Street wins for charm. Every year most of the houses on Christmas Street (otherwise known as Glen Arbor Street) are brightly lit up with a thematic display of Christmas cheer. Glen Arbor is located off of 1500 East and just south of 1700 South.

The rest of the year, the street is quiet. The homes are modest in size and style, mostly in what is called a "World War II cottage." This style was created according to the guidelines recommended by the FHA, which hoped to enable the American dream of home ownership, national security in the wake of the world war, and suburban neighborhoods. There is something so quintessentially American about the houses and the street itself—it represents the components of this dream in physical form. The holiday celebration that brings together the residents of this little street is also characteristic of the American experience: We love to join together to celebrate our values, traditions, and memories.

The walking paths through Red Butte Garden are lined with the region's most popular plants that are indigenous or thrive in dry desert environments. Summer concerts bring thousands of locals to Red Butte—another advantage of living so close to natural environments at the foothills of the Wasatch Mountains.

Left: "Pachyderm" describes elephants, rhinoceroses, and hippopotamuses, and the Pachyderm House has long been a zoo favorite, as seen here circa 1950s. *Top:* Jungle cat sculptures peer down on the zoo entrance in this mid-century postcard.

HOGLE ZOO

Located in Liberty Park, Salt Lake City's first "zoo" initially was a bit limited in its array, featuring just a deer and a cage of monkeys in 1911. But the simple collection sparked the enthusiasm of a group who vigorously promoted the concept of a city zoo. With that in mind, and $153 to spend, the next year the Salt Lake Parks Department launched a zoo that featured a pair of golden pheasants, Mandarin ducks, foxes, squirrels, white storks, blue peafowl, and white-faced monkeys.

In 1931, Mr. and Mrs. James Hogle donated acreage at the mouth of Emigration Canyon for a zoo, and the Salt Lake Zoological Society formed to raise funds. On July 31 of that year, the Hogle Zoo opened to a crowd of more than 14,000 people. Despite the strains of the Great Depression, the zoo expanded over the next several decades to include a range of animals from different ecosystems, from lions and apes to seals and hippos. Renowned Utah sculptor Dr. Avard Fairbanks's 1947 sculpture of two mountain lions sitting atop 18-foot-tall columns mark the east entrance to the zoo.

Throughout its history, Hogle Zoo's principal draw has been its animal displays (such as these rhinos, at right), but it also must keep abreast of national trends. To that effect, the zoo has added a small train that runs along the children's petting zoo area, concessions, gift shops, picnic areas, and most recently, the Conservation Carousel. In 2008, Salt Lake voters supported Proposition #2 "Renew the Zoo," which allocated funds for zoo exhibit improvements. The zoo gates are seen below in 2009.

COMING TO AMERICA

Salt Lake City was a city socially divided for many years. The east and west sides of town became physical boundaries, dictating the differences between people of varying religions, economic classes, and ethnicities. After 1847, many people filtered through the historic Pioneer Fort situated at 300 West and 300 South. Some were simply travelers passing through the state. Many of them stopped in Union Square west of Main Street and Temple Square for supplies and to simply rest a spell.

The advent of the railroad in 1870 unleashed a new flood of immigrants, lured to Utah by the promise of the American dream: wealth, security, and the hope of a new life. Their intent was to find a job, earn money to support their relatives back home, and pinpoint the elusive security that had escaped them in the past.

COMMUNITY LIVING

As the Westside flourished from the 1880s through the 1920s, the district became known as one whose inhabitants were very diverse. As a group, immigrants were a ready workforce: Pushed out of their homes by a variety of forces—social dislocation, poverty, political unrest—they were pulled to Utah by the promise of finding work laboring for the rapidly opening mines,

mills, smelters, and railroads. Naturally, neighborhoods sprung up around these business districts. Many of Salt Lake City's ethnic groups—notably the Greeks, Japanese, Italians, and people of Slavic descent—lived in apartments, ran small family businesses, and settled in clusters soon known as "Greek Town," "Little Italy," and "Japan Town" (also known as *Nihonmachi*). In these neighborhoods, immigrants appropriated the industrial spaces and reworked them as homes for families or single men who were working until they could afford to send home for their wives and families.

The Westside looked different from the rest of the city—industrial complexes mixed with adobe or frame houses, boarding houses, and restaurants to serve the mobile population of new workers

Students gather outside the Japanese Church of Christ in this mid-20th century photo.

Left: Swimmers are extremely buoyant in the Great Salt Lake because of the 12 percent salinity. Saltair is shown in the distance in this 1908 photo.

who planned to stay in town only temporarily. Immigrants first roomed in boarding houses near the railroad depots, where they found agents recruiting for work in the mines or smelters, the railroad, or on farms. As time went on and workers decided to lay down roots, they made their homes here, planting vegetable gardens and erecting tent villages and crowded shanties. These early immigrant populations acquired the space not only for survival but also as a means to develop a sense of community. The boundaries that defined these neighborhoods were formed by familiarity as well as segregation. Although this differentiation was partly about escalating land prices and the haves versus the have-nots, it was also about a growing separation between private and public life and the compartmentalization of residential neighborhoods.

Dahlias surround the Mexico monument at the International Peace Gardens.

TOGETHER IN PRAISE

Immigrant congregations built 25 churches on the Westside between 1889 and 1950. These churches were immensely important to the community. For example, built in 1925, the Holy Trinity Greek Orthodox Church was the community center of the two blocks that formed Greek Town. The church served as the scene of many weddings, graduations, and funerals. There, Greek immigrants found comfort within a city that at the time embraced a particular type of person defined in both religion and ethnicity.

In the wake of World War II, the Commission on Wartime Relocation and Internment of Civilians efforts were headquartered in Salt Lake City, as was the Salt Lake Buddhist Temple. Salt Lake City's Westside Japan Town neighborhood was central to Western American efforts to find new homes and jobs and start life anew for Japanese American families relocated during the war.

During the 1970s, much of this historic landscape of ethnic enclaves and neighborhood businesses made way for the construction of the new Salt Palace along West Temple and between 100 South and 200 South. What historically had been the scene of Japanese laundries, noodle restaurants, and boarding houses later became a big-box convention center. Within decades, the only reminders of the richly diverse

landscape of Japan Town were the Salt Lake Buddhist Temple and the Japanese Church of Christ. Many elderly residents of the neighborhood were moved to a new city-built high-rise apartment building at 200 West and 100 South. Rather than moving as a community, most Japanese businesses and families relocated one by one to other parts of the city and assimilated into new neighborhoods.

GATEWAY TO SALT LAKE CITY

For the past decade, the Westside neighborhood surrounding the railroad depots has been called The Gateway. In the old days, this area of Salt Lake City formed a threshold to the rest of the city for new immigrants and settlers. Today, it is the passageway that visitors travel through on their way from the airport to downtown. This neighborhood includes 64 ten-acre blocks, stretching west from West Temple to 1000 West and from North Temple to 900 South. There, one may find businesses and buildings that express the urban nature of the area, from industrial complexes and railroad depots to homeless shelters and soup kitchens. Hip warehouse conversions bring a new urban chic population to this neighborhood, with coffee shops, art galleries, and an eclectic collection of small shops. Cultural neighborhoods stretch toward the west in the shadow of sound walls built on both sides of the freeway, which cuts a swath through the landscape some longtime residents call home.

Blending the old with the new, The Gateway's fountain is surrounded by modern structures that mimic a historic streetscape on a grand scale.

THE FARMERS MARKET

A PERFECT EXAMPLE OF Salt Lake City's "Buy Local First" campaign, the incredibly successful Farmers Market brings farmers, artisans, and restaurants to Pioneer Park. Every Saturday morning from June through the end of October, locals gather at the market, where just about any type of produce that is in season is available. Buyers can also peruse the plethora of arts and crafts, from jewelry and handmade creams to leather belts and tie-dye scarves. More than 60 Utah artists sell their handcrafted goods, and more than 80 farmers proudly display their freshest crops, including boxes of ripe and juicy tomatoes, fresh flowers sold out of the back of a truck, and piles upon piles of corn on the cob.

The Farmers Market is a vibrant event that draws people of every age—families picnic and lazily lounge in the sunshine as acoustic musicians and street performers entertain the children. A special dog park gives restless canines the chance to run around in a safe fenced-in area. Despite its other amenities, such as tennis courts, a bocce ball court, and walking paths, for many years, Pioneer Park's ten acres were primarily used by the homeless and drug dealers. Nearly two decades ago, the Downtown Alliance launched the Farmers Market as a way of reinvigorating the park and bringing people from across the valley downtown each weekend. In 2009, the Farmers Market celebrated its 17th anniversary. Every year, the market gets more crowded and popular—recently a valet service has been added, as well as additional hours on Tuesday evenings. People find the market to be a fun activity whether they are by themselves or with friends or family.

Carrots and other produce are piled high at the Farmers Market.

RAILROAD DEPOTS AND THE INTERMODAL HUB

For an immigrant coming into Salt Lake City for the first time, the Denver and Rio Grande Railroad Depot would have been a grand threshold symbolic of the promise held by the American dream. It mattered less that outside the depot the land was crowded with warehouses and industrial complexes—in the depot, anything seemed possible. This structure (built in 1911) continues to make a commanding presence in Salt Lake City's Westside neighborhood.

Built in 1909, the Union Pacific Depot shares a similar feeling. During its period of greatest use, stained glass windows and gas lamps helped create a lively, elegant, and compelling architecture. Again, as the entry to the city, the depot set the tone for what came next: Salt Lake City was a place of growing sophistication and opportunity, definitely worth the time it would take to explore. Today, it is used for offices, as well as a restaurant and music venue called, fittingly, The Depot.

For years, Amtrak searched for a permanent home in Salt Lake City, first at the Union Pacific Depot in 1971 and then the Rio Grande in 1986. Finally, in 1999, the company moved to a temporary "shack" that would later become the Intermodal Hub. On July 5, 2005, the city dedicated the new Intermodal Hub building; within three years, the Greyhound bus terminal had moved on the site. The Utah Transit Authority (UTA) began regular bus service to the Hub and on April 26, 2008, UTA offered FrontRunner commuter rail service and TRAX light rail service. The Intermodal Hub makes public transportation a viable and convenient solution for many who live in the suburbs and work downtown or at the university.

Top: The lobby of the Denver and Rio Grande Railroad Depot is shown in 1912. *Bottom:* The Rio Grande sign still soars above the buildings. Today, the depot is home to the Utah State Historical Society and the Utah Arts Council.

ALL ABOARD!

The Utah Transit Authority launched its FrontRunner commuter rail line on April 26, 2008. It travels the 38 miles between Salt Lake City and Ogden. The Intermodal Hub demonstrates and perpetuates sustainable values, such as brownfield redevelopment, alternative transportation, water-efficient landscaping, recycled content, optimized energy performance, and low-emitting materials and landscape. Adding retail, parking, and a permanent Amtrak station are future goals. *Counterclockwise, from top right:* A FrontRunner commuter train passes The Gateway; the train stops at the Intermodal Hub; and the Union Pacific station is lit up with holiday lights.

THE WAREHOUSE DISTRICT

The Keyser Warehouse was part of the Warehouse District. The building is shown here in this tax photo from the mid-1930s.

Capitalizing on the proximity of railroad spurs that made for easy transportation of his wholesale produce, in 1898, Wilber E. Henderson located the headquarters of his statewide wholesale grocery business in what would become known as the Warehouse District. He hired one of the most prominent local architects, Walter E. Ware, to design a handsome three-story warehouse. But Henderson's was just one of many warehouses that sprang up. Another was the Keyser Warehouse; ads ran in the newspaper advertising, "The Better Class of People store their furniture at the Keyser Fireproof Warehouse."

In 1910, the Free Farmers Market began on Pierpont Avenue between 300 and 400 West. In the early 1980s, an artist co-operative called Artspace leased the space and reconfigured it as an eclectic artists' studio and apartment space. They also reclaimed the blighted land to the rear for a community garden and spearheaded the revitalization of the nearby Warehouse District to the west. The district's makeover as a "mixed-use" space, including The Gateway, has made it a very popular area, offering an array of lofts, restaurants, shops, bars, and clubs.

The first Challenge Cream & Butter Association opened in Los Angeles in 1911, selling dairy products from creamery associations in the region. The Salt Lake City shop is shown above in 1938. Grocery and produce businesses lined the streets in the Warehouse District, a distinctive commercial activity dependent on the close proximity of the railroad.

As a mixed-use development, The Gateway offers a range of attractions from movie theaters to popular restaurants, and shops large and small. An outdoor shopping mall at heart, the Gateway's low-cost housing and upscale condos provide a range of residential alternatives with the advantage of downtown living.

THE GATEWAY

Above: A residence complex stands tall at The Gateway, as seen here in 2008. The complex runs parallel to 500 South, a street the city is converting into a boulevard featuring native, drought-tolerant landscaping, winding paths that run in sinuous lines, and inviting benches for pedestrians to pause and enjoy the sunshine. *Right:* There's nothing like playing in a cool fountain on a hot day. During the summer, the Olympic fountain blasts water vertically into the air, choreographed to the Olympic theme song and other music such as "America the Beautiful."

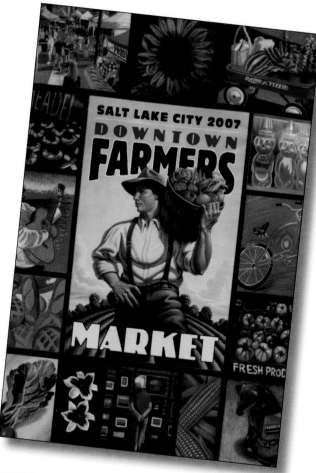

PIONEER PARK

Two weeks after arriving in the Salt Lake Valley in 1847, the pioneers set about building a fort. Although it was a hot, dry August, they wisely anticipated that winter would be upon them before they knew it. Using adobe bricks fashioned out of soil and water, they built walls seven to nine feet tall and two to three feet thick at the base. In the fort, the roof slanted slightly into the center courtyard area. When it rained that first fall, water streamed in through leaks in the makeshift roof—so much so that Zina Diantha Young recorded in her journal that she held up an umbrella all night to protect her sleeping children. Mud pressed between cracks in the wall turned to dust, making it impossible to keep the room or the children clean.

It wasn't luxury living, but 160 families could live in the fort at a time, providing the settlers much-needed shelter after the difficult journey through the Rocky Mountains. In Heber C. Kimball's room on December 9, 1848, church leaders gathered to organize the provincial State of Deseret. The first territorial government elections were held in the adobe school constructed at the center of the fort.

In 1898, the city named the block "Pioneer Park." A public swimming pool and playground was built there during the Progressive Era. More recently, the Downtown Alliance has staged a Farmers Market at Pioneer Park from June through October—one of the most effective community building traditions to date.

The Downtown Alliance's mission is to "build a dynamic and diverse community that is the regional center for culture, commerce, and entertainment." The popularity of the Farmers Market at Pioneer Park (as seen above left, in 2009) attests to their remarkable success. Local farmers drive their trucks up to the 300 South edge of Pioneer Park and sell their products out of the back.

Left: A woman stands outside the Japanese Church of Christ in this undated photo. *Above:* In 1962, the church constructed a new Christian education building for the *Sansei,* or third generation Japanese Americans. The Japanese Church of Christ is seen here in 2009.

JAPANESE CHURCH OF CHRIST

Japanese immigrants arrived in Utah in the 1880s to work on the railroad or in agriculture. The 1900 census recorded 417 Japanese people living in Utah, but by 1920 that number had surged to 3,000. During that time, as the West expanded, Presbyterian, Methodist, and other Protestant groups traveled to western towns, concentrating on converting new members and establishing missions. The Japanese immigrants included both Buddhists and converted Christians, but it wasn't until 1918 that the Japanese Church of Christ at 268 West 100 South opened in Salt Lake City.

The effort came about through the collaboration of Congregational and Japanese churches along the Pacific Coast. Representing the group, Reverend M. Kobayashi and Reverend H. Toyotome came to Utah to do missionary work. There they founded a Sunday school and a Bible class. The Japanese Church of Christ, along with the Salt Lake Buddhist Temple, was once part of a thriving cultural area in Salt Lake City. Dubbed *Nihonmachi* or "Japan Town," it was the historic center of the immigrant neighborhood, full of noodle restaurants, laundries, and boarding houses that catered to the city's Japanese population. The neighborhood took a hit in the mid-1960s when many of its businesses were razed to build the new Salt Palace. Although the single-story Japanese Church of Christ is modest in size, it continues to provide a haven for Salt Lake City Christians.

Since 1952, the Japanese Church of Christ's annual fundraiser, the Aki Matsuri (or Fall Festival) does more than raise money—it also displays Japanese culture to the city, featuring dancing, martial arts, and various art and food demonstrations. In this photo, drummers perform during the festival.

JAPANESE RELOCATION EFFORTS

THREE MONTHS AFTER the attack on Pearl Harbor, on February 19, 1942, President Franklin Roosevelt created a civilian agency called the War Relocation Authority to remove all persons of Japanese ancestry from states bordering the Pacific coastline, including California, Oregon, Washington, and part of Arizona and other West Coast areas.

Topaz, located in the desert near Delta, was the principal Utah camp for internees. One Topaz internee was the Reverend Kenryo Kumata from San Francisco, the head of the Buddhist Churches of America. After his release, Kumata established a Buddhist Church in the Utah towns of Ogden, Honeyville, Deweyville, Garand, and Corinne. In fact, many members of Utah's Japanese American community first came to the state as relocates; most lived in Salt Lake City or Ogden as well as a few farming towns throughout the region. In Salt Lake City, Japanese Americans congregated in Japan Town. Salt Lake City's relocation center was located at 318 Atlas Building; relocation officer E. Rex Lee helped those who chose to stay in Utah after the war find new jobs and homes. In 1947, the Alien Land Act was repealed and Japanese citizens could once again purchase land. Because of the Evacuation Indemnity Claims Act in 1948, however, less than 10 percent of the loss experienced by those sent to internment camps—their careers, homes, belongings, and reputations—was ever repaid.

A bugle corps plays at a Japanese internment camp in the 1940s.

SALT LAKE BUDDHIST TEMPLE

Salt Lake City's first Buddhist congregation met in the main hall of the Kyushuya Hotel at 168 West South Temple until a new temple was built in 1924 (shown here in 2009).

Outside of this unassuming building at 211 West 100 South, only a slight decorative detail hints at the Buddhist rituals performed within: A projecting portico resembling a Shinto shrine pitches outward over the doorway. Inside, practitioners chant and reflect as incense wafts through the air. Three golden altars are within the chapel; in the center altar is a golden statue of Amida Buddha, reminding Buddhists of the importance of compassion.

Life was hard for many people entering the untamed West, and especially so for those who toiled to create routes of transportation between the fledgling cities and towns. Many early Japanese immigrants worked on railroads and in mines, and many died as a result of their labor. In 1912, a minister from San Francisco held a memorial service in Ogden, Utah, to honor these first-generation (or *Issei)* immigrants. The event sparked interest in forming a Buddhist temple in Salt Lake City. That year, Reverend Kenryo Kuwahara served as the church's first minister. Located across the street from the Japanese Church of Christ in what was once known as Japan Town, the Salt Lake Buddhist Temple continues to serve as an important community institution.

BEING BUDDHIST IN SALT LAKE CITY

Above: Mourners stand outside the Buddhist Temple for a 1949 funeral. *Left:* A man worships in the temple in 1938. Starting in 1918, Reverend Renjo Hirozawa offered Sunday School classes designed to educate *Nisei,* or second-generation, Japanese youth about their parent's religious traditions. Life for the *Issei,* or first generation, had been tough. These men and women worked difficult, underpaid jobs and had made sacrifices to establish their families in the American West. Many believed that supressing their Buddhist traditions would help their children assimilate more easily. Eventually this mode of thought changed, and the Buddhist Temple Sunday School became an important agent of the socialization process and formation of Japanese American identity.

HOLY TRINITY GREEK ORTHODOX CHURCH

Photographs help us remember how profoundly different the blocks near the Denver and Rio Grande and Union Pacific Railroad depots were around the turn of the 19th century. Diverse, densely built ethnic neighborhoods housed men who came to Utah to work in the mines of Carbon or Emery counties or to work in local industries. Like so many others, Greek men were lured to Utah by the wealth promised in the mines and railroad construction.

In Salt Lake City, Greek Town was founded near the Denver and Rio Grande Depot, not far from the current location of The Gateway. There, Greek coffeehouses offered companionship and social life, as well as coffee, candy, pastries, and native products familiar to the Greek palate—dried octopus, Turkish tobacco, olive oil, goat cheese, figs, and dates. By 1924, the Greek community included the wives and children who had followed their husbands and fathers. In 1925, the Holy Trinity Greek Orthodox Church was built to replace an earlier, and far smaller, building.

Prominent Utah architects Theodore Pope and Harold Burton used the Greek cross as inspiration for the church's plan and the Byzantine style for the opulent exterior decoration. Inside, the congregation is seated facing an altar positioned toward the rising sun—the source of light and symbolic of Christ— as is traditional in Greek Orthodox churches.

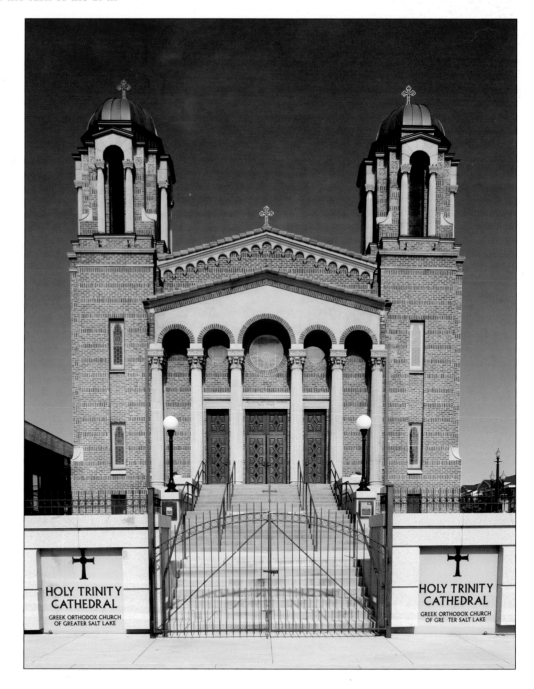

Holy Trinity Greek Orthodox Church, also known as Holy Trinity Cathedral, is shown here in 2009.

Top left: A new, larger Holy Trinity was built in 1925. It is shown here in the mid-20th century. *Bottom left:* The original Greek church is pictured here in 1908. Greek Town emerged around the area where Holy Trinity now stands at the corner of 300 West and 300 South, although today none of the original Greek coffeehouses or boardinghouses remain.

A group of men pose at a funeral in 1908. A series of iconic pictures run along the space behind the altar.

THE NELSON WHEELER WHIPPLE HOUSE

One of the earliest surviving pioneer-era houses in the city, the two-story adobe home built by Nelson Wheeler Whipple was constructed, brick by brick, in 1854. When first built, the building had a central staircase and two rooms on each side on both floors, which maximized the interior space of what is basically a rectangular box. Much of what went into the making of the house is well known because Whipple kept detailed records of its construction, which used "about 25,000 adobes, about 7,000 feet of lumber, and 10,000 shingles."

In Utah, adobe bricks were fashioned to look like kiln-dried bricks, and they were used for the homes of all social classes. Even Brigham Young used adobe in the construction of the Beehive House. Made with the most basic materials—dirt and water, and sometimes with straw added for additional strength—virtually every small town in the region had its own adobe yard where whole families gathered to stomp the mud into the right consistency. They would then press the material into adobe molds that were laid out to dry in the sun for two weeks. Adobe buildings were inexpensive to build, had a ready source of materials, and were great insulators. Adobe walls, like those at the Whipple house, were typically three bricks thick and efficient at keeping homes toasty warm in the winter and cool in the summer months—both requisite in the varied seasons of Utah Territory.

Signature Books restored the Nelson Wheeler Whipple House in 1992 for its editorial offices. The building is seen here in recent times.

The Nelson Wheeler Whipple House, shown here in this 1936 tax photo, is one of many Salt Lake City homes to be fashioned out of adobe bricks.

LEO MONTOYA BOXING CLUB

For more than 50 years, Leo Montoya has trained local boxers for two hours daily in a century-old building—the Leo Montoya Boxing Club.

Montoya, a boxer who won a gold medal at the Pan American Games in 1949, began his training career in 1953 in Helper, Utah, with a group of about 45 kids (including six of his own sons). Back then, Montoya's "gym" was a vacant lot where he hung a punching bag on a tree limb and led the prospective boxers in calisthenics. Montoya bought the current gym facility at 246 North 600 West in 1960; prior to that the building had been used as a meat market, a television store, and a secondhand shop. Throughout his career, Montoya has trained many boxing champs, and he has taken more than 100 fighters to regional tournaments.

Leo Montoya Boxing Club is a community institution, bar none. While Montoya's goal is to produce competitive boxers, the club also fosters strong values in area kids, not only for commitment and hard work, but also community and charity.

Though small in size, the Leo Montoya Boxing Club (shown here circa 1960) has had a major impact on the neighborhood and its inhabitants. The club has served as a place to build character as well as physical strength.

Leo Montoya (shown here in 2009) and his wife Rebecca raised 11 children in Salt Lake City's Westside. This local legend was described by the *Deseret News* as a "prototypical gym rat."

Right: Fairgoers stroll in this photo from 1909. Besides the fair, visitors could see experimental farms, newfangled products, and the exotic animal breeds or botanical wonders that were on display. What's more, it was the perfect networking opportunity for farmers, who were accustomed to living in remote locations far from their nearest neighbor. *Below:* Children in wooden shoes pose in front of the McDonald Candy Company Dutch Chocolates display in 1907.

UTAH STATE FAIRPARK

Everyone loves a fair, and Utahans are no different. In 1856, the Deseret Agricultural and Manufacturing Society organized to hold annual expositions in Salt Lake City that celebrated the domestic arts and home manufacturing in the name of territorial self-sufficiency.

During the 1880s, the territorial legislature investigated more permanent sites for the Fairpark. Before it was moved to its present site in 1902, the fair was held at the Tenth Ward Square, the site of Trolley Square and Market Row at 100 South and West Temple. The earliest fairs coincided with the October General Conference of the LDS church. Instead of today's traditional blue ribbons, diplomas were awarded for excellence, with the words "Holiness to the Lord," and symbolic pictures of a beehive and the All-Seeing Eye across the top. Many religious elements were removed from the event after it became known as the State Fair in 1907.

Located today along the banks of the Jordan River, the Fairpark is the site of the annual Utah State Fair. It also features more than 300,000 square feet of open space, ideal for picnics, outdoor concerts, and other events.

Top: A large sign advertises the fair's highlights. The annual Utah State Fair brings together the city's diverse families to celebrate the state's best agricultural production, listen to music, and enjoy bumper cars to their hearts' content.
Left: The Sheep Barn is one of the most unusual buildings at the Fairpark. Two huge garage doors provide entry for trucks hauling sheep into the structure for display during the fair.

POPLAR GROVE

Pioneers settled in Poplar Grove (located near what is now 900 West and 100 South) in the 1850s. Since then, a vibrant community has flourished in this Westside neighborhood, one marked by ethnic and religious diversity. The first generation of settlers to Poplar Grove included George Q. Cannon, an LDS church apostle. Cannon's elaborate Victorian home included a secret staircase and hiding place where he and other polygamists would hide from the federal police during the underground period of the 1880s. William Clayton, author of the sentimental pioneer hymn, "Come, Come Ye Saints," also lived in Poplar Grove.

By the turn of the 20th century, Italians, Greeks, Syrians, Lebanese, and other ethnic groups had homes in the neighborhood. Hispanics, Pacific Islanders, Vietnamese, Hmong, and other arrivals created even greater diversity. The area architecture is also eclectic, featuring a range of styles from Queen Anne cottages and bungalows to mid-20th century World War II houses. Key neighborhood institutions include the Chapman Library, the International Peace Gardens and Jordan Park, the University Neighborhood Partners, and the Guadalupe School.

Counterclockwise from top: The Jordan River is calm on this day in 2009; an example of the type of modest bungalow typically found in Poplar Grove is shown in an undated photo; children walk outside the Poplar Grove School in 1916.

ROSE PARK

The Rose Park neighborhood in Salt Lake City's Westside personifies the values perpetuated by the Federal Housing Administration (FHA) after 1934: sensible family living in carefully designed, modest-size homes. The surest guarantee to America's future in the wake of World War II was to situate its returning vets in homes, and it was the job of the FHA to show them how they might best live. In fact, when it was first built, virtually all the homeowners in Rose Park were veterans of the war.

The typical postwar cottage prescribed by the FHA moved away from the excesses of earlier generations of American homes, offering greater financial and spatial economy. For decades, the FHA produced pattern books that featured a series of housing types designed to meet the particular needs of families with a single child or more. In cookie-cutter fashion, these houses offered pretty much the same plan: one or two stories, with two or three bedrooms, a living room entered from the front door, bedrooms toward the back, and a kitchen with a window over the sink so mothers could observe their children playing during the day.

Although originally a homogeneous neighborhood, today Rose Park is a very diverse part of the city both ethnically as well as religiously. It's also known for its beautiful golf course—featuring a bed of roses planted behind the 10th tee.

For the family of a returning World War II vet, an FHA home (such as this one circa 1950) was the symbol of the American dream: a single-family detached home with all the modern conveniences possible and a yard on a safe street in a subdivision devoted to young families.

Multi-unit apartment structures and large-scale governmental office buildings are found on major arteries bordering the neighborhood, such as this apartment complex in 1965.

A family poses on a bridge in the International Peace Gardens in this undated photograph.

Marking the 2002 Olympic Games, these posts represent the countries that sent athletes to compete. Each says "May Peace Prevail on Earth" in a different language.

INTERNATIONAL PEACE GARDENS

Since it was conceived in 1939, the International Peace Gardens symbolize the effort to find peace and bridge the gap in understanding between the nations of the world. Located in Jordan Park, on the bank of the Jordan River, the Peace Gardens was finally dedicated in 1952.

Reflecting the cultural diversity found in Salt Lake City's Westside neighborhood, the park pays tribute to 28 nations with flora native to their regions and garden architecture and statuary representing their unique environments. Visitors can find flags, symbols, statues, windmills, pagodas, and even Viking tombs. The gardens are also a popular picnic ground and backdrop for weddings and memorials. Various cultural events, including the Norwegian Independence Day parade, are also held there.

The Chinese monument includes this pagoda (seen here in 2009), with an entrance framed by two guardian lions, a meandering walking path, and a bridge.

The Swiss monument at the International Peace Gardens was dedicated on August 14, 1965. It includes a Swiss chalet, a looming concrete model of the Matterhorn mountain, and edelweiss flowers in the surrounding garden.

The largest percentage of Utah's 19th-century immigrant population came from the British Isles. This monument to Wales was dedicated on September 8, 1971.

SALTAIR

After the arrival of the railroad in 1870, and the ease of transportation that it allowed, great enthusiasm prevailed over the notion of exploiting the Great Salt Lake's shorelines for recreation and entertainment. On January 14, 1893, the *Deseret News* announced construction of a new lake resort called Saltair that was destined for world renown "wherever newspapers are read or words transmitted by lightening."

The Mormon Church was the principal stockholder of the new company. The idea behind Saltair was to provide a wholesome alternative to "pleasure resorts" that exposed young people to "the villainous arts of practice voluptuaries." The church hired architect Richard K. A. Kletting to design the main pavilion. Built on a platform over the water, Saltair featured onion domes and towers that conjured images of a Middle Eastern mosque.

In its first year in 1893, more than 100,000 visitors enjoyed the resort's beaches, picnic areas, restaurants, and amusement park rides. By 1919, the number had reached 450,000. The rail fare to Saltair was inexpensive, which made it possible for all social classes to enjoy the resort's many water activities, dances, and performances.

Saltair's builders hoped the recreation area could be both an amusement park and a safe and healthy environment for area youth. It became known as the Coney Island of Utah Territory. Saltair is seen here in recent times.

A terrible fire destroyed Saltair's first pavilion on April 22, 1925. The pavilion (shown here mid-reconstruction circa 1925) included the world's largest dance floor at the time.

Near the shores of the Great Salt Lake rise piles of white pillowed foam. According to Utah's Geological Survey, these mounds are not related to the high salt content of the water but to surfactants that appear from natural processes in the lake. The phenomenon is shown here in this undated photo.

Saltair's boardwalk gave visitors the chance to stroll comfortably along the Great Salt Lake on a wooden walkway suspended more than three feet above the water, as shown in this photo circa 1901. Gazebos located along the way provided shady spots in the summer months.

FRUIT TREES AND WARM SPRINGS

Salt Lake City's grid never corresponded to the square plan of the plat of the City of Zion. Instead, nine blocks moved to the south of Temple Square and only a few blocks moved to the north. Even so, and despite the hilly terrain, the area just north of the Temple Block became a favorite area for settlement. One- and two-room adobe houses were built upon the hillside to house the city's earliest residents who were, for the most part, working-class Mormon immigrants. The location offered both an immediate proximity to nearby Main Street and a break from the noise and commotion of downtown.

This area, eventually known as Capitol Hill for the Capitol building overlooking downtown, has always been a dense, predominantly residential district. But Capitol Hill is actually comprised of a group of smaller districts—Marmalade Hill, Wasatch Springs, and Arsenal Hill. A high degree of social diversity contributes to the neighborhood's distinctiveness. It's also physically different, including adobe, brick, and frame buildings; high foundations and retaining walls; oddly shaped blocks; and a chaotic street pattern. Even the orientation of dwellings to the street is different—houses were built much closer to the street than the 20-foot setbacks more commonly found elsewhere in the city.

ORCHARDS WERE PLENTIFUL

As was true throughout Utah Territory, water sources determined where settlement occurred. For decades, houses sat on large lots more reminiscent of rural neighborhoods than the city. Orchards stretched toward the backs of these lots. Even though most of the residents were not farmers, the orchards allowed them a certain measure of self-sufficiency. The orchards provided the names of the streets in the Marmalade Hill district: Apricot, Quince, and Almond. These streets are far narrower than those found elsewhere in the city, clinging to the sides of steeply climbing hills and closely lined with charming pioneer and Victorian cottages.

Above: The West High School football team practices in 1905. West High is ranked Utah's number-one high school.

Left: The Utah State Capitol towers over the neighborhood, as seen in this photo from 1995.

On Main Street at the top edge of the neighborhood, there are blocks of dignified Craftsman–style houses marking the transition northeast toward the Capitol Hill neighborhood. Visual diversity is the core feature of the Marmalade District, a parade of historical styles built close to the city's civic, religious, and commercial core. The neighborhood offers stylish and impressive homes within blocks of amenities—an important feature for the city workers and professionals living here, for whom convenience and accessibility are premiere virtues. The rich diversity of housing found in the Marmalade District contrasts significantly with the larger, more stylish buildings immediately to the east.

The Mormon Battalion Monument is located on the southeast section of the front lawn of the Utah State Capitol. The piece was created by artist Gilbert Griswold in 1927 to honor the 500 Mormon pioneers who volunteered with the U.S. army during the Mexican War.

DISASTER!

Because of its close proximity to downtown, fabulous views of the valley, and the Great Salt Lake beyond, Capitol Hill became one of the most desirable locations in town. After the arrival of the railroad in 1870, non-Mormon railroad and mining entrepreneurs chose to settle on the hill, diversifying what historically had been a predominantly Latter-day Saints population.

During the 19th century, the Mormon inhabitants of Salt Lake City had an ongoing conflicted relationship with the federal government. Arsenal Hill was the place they stored their arms in the event of a conflict with local Native Americans or even the possibility of a confrontation with the U.S. government. In perhaps the most dramatic event to occur on the site, an accidental explosion of blasting powder in April 1876 made the city reconsider the location of the storage facility so close to the city. The *Deseret Evening News* reported the event: "TERRIBLE DISASTER—Terrible Explosion of Forty Tons of Powder—Four Persons Immediately Killed and Others Injured—Great Damage to Property." The arsenal was shut down.

Found at the top slope of State Street near the crest of the hill, the area eventually became the place where wealthy businessmen built some of the most beautiful homes in the city. The Kensington at 180 North Main (built in 1906) and the Kestler at 264 and 268 North State (built in 1915) are extant apartment buildings from the period when the Capitol was built.

TAKING THE PLUNGE

Before the Mormon pioneers arrived in the valley, a small party of advance scouts was sent to the area, and they located hot springs that today sit just north of downtown. It was the close proximity of the waters, renamed Wasatch Springs, that played a part in the decision of Mormon leaders to settle in the area. Brigham Young noted that the water would make a fine source to power mills. He also commented that it was hot enough to scald a hog. For some time, Wasatch Springs was a popular spa and recreational spot, but in 1946, the State Health Department deemed the place a safety hazard because of high amounts of bacteria in the pools. The city began chlorinating the pools in 1949, but by 1970, Wasatch Springs was completely closed.

THE EFFECTS OF SPRAWL

As was true for other historic neighborhoods near the center of the city, Capitol Hill was hurt by the flight to the suburbs in the decades following World War II. By that time, some houses in the Marmalade and Capitol Hill districts were a century old and showed their age. By the 1960s, yards that were once landscaped with flowers were now filled with weeds and garbage. High-rise condominium complexes built in the 1970s contrasted with the quirky character of the historic buildings native to the neighborhood, but they also offered new downtown housing alternatives.

During the past decades, lovers of historic homes have begun the process of revitalizing these neighborhoods,

Flower beds add a ripple of color in front of Council Hall, as seen here.

remodeling homes that had been subdivided into multiple apartments and restoring the buildings to their original single-family home configuration. Importantly, the Capitol Hill and Marmalade neighborhoods are now known as some of the most socially diverse sections of the city, distinctive for their architectural and landscape variety—a sort of urban chic hipness that contrasts with the more staid suburban neighborhoods on the southern edge of the city. At night, dominated by views of the newly restored, brightly lit Capitol building, the area is noted for its fantastic views of the city and the natural environment beyond, divergent street patterns, and easy accessibility to both light rail and walking paths that lead into nearby canyons.

The Utah State Capitol is under construction in this photo from May 1914.

Men celebrate the last stone used for the building of the Capitol in February 1915. Completed ahead of schedule, the dedication of the Utah State Capitol was held on October 9, 1916.

UTAH STATE CAPITOL

Regardless of how many skyscrapers spring up along the Salt Lake landscape, the Utah State Capitol and the Salt Lake Temple still compete for most distinctive local landmark. Perfectly situated on Capitol Hill at the north end of State Street, the Capitol is an example of classically influenced architecture, featuring symmetry, formality, and a central dome. Utah architect Richard K. A. Kletting won the commission to design the building, and construction began on December 26, 1912.

The interior of the Capitol building is enlivened by more than 200 pieces of art, the majority by Utah artists. Most prominent are the immense murals—each 4,500-square-foot canvas features scenes from Utah history: Father Escalante first entering Utah Valley in 1776; Peter Skene Ogden at the Ogden River in 1828; John C. Frémont's visit to the Great Salt Lake in 1843; and the familiar image of Brigham Young and the Utah pioneers entering the valley of the Great Salt Lake in 1847.

Outdoor statuary also depicts key moments in state history. In particular is a piece by Utah sculptor Cyrus Dallin showing Massassoit, chief of the Wampanoags, who welcomed the Pilgrims to Plymouth Rock. Controversial because it did not represent Utah's own Native American peoples, the statue nevertheless assumes a prominent position in the Capitol's front yard.

Almost a century after it was built, the Utah State Capitol (shown here in 1999) went through an extensive $260 million restoration project to seismically upgrade the building and preserve the interior and exterior art and furnishings.

Murals on the rotunda walls were painted by artists in 1935. Painted on the interior surface of the dome itself are seagulls, like those that fly over the Great Salt Lake.

RICHARD K. A. KLETTING

This "Dean of Utah Architecture" designed the Utah State Capitol building, the McIntyre Building, the State Mental Hospital, and countless houses and public buildings throughout the city. Born in Württemberg, Germany, in 1858, Richard K. A. Kletting came to Utah in the 1880s. As a boy, he traveled to Paris, where he was exposed to the most up-to-date and technologically advanced architecture; later he was trained in engineering and architectural technology in Germany and France.

A decade after he first arrived in Utah, he received the commission for the design of Saltair, a swimming and dance resort on the banks of the Great Salt Lake. Equally facile at all the most current architectural styles, Kletting chose to design Saltair with a Middle Eastern flair, an exotic design complete with onion domes more evocative of Persia than provincial Utah. Influenced by the architecture of the World's Columbian Exposition of 1893, Kletting revealed his talent for capturing the essence of a project and communicating it in the forms and details of a particularly appropriate architectural style. Perhaps his most important commission was the Utah State Capitol, a job he won through a design competition. His design for the renaissance revival–style stone building located at the top of State Street, mirrored the colonnades, domed rotundas, symmetry, and formality so typical of public governmental architecture at the time.

The Old Council Hall is seen here circa 1870.

In 1961, Council Hall was dismantled. Each of the 325 sandstone slabs were taken apart, numbered, and moved to the new site, where they were reconstructed.

COUNCIL HALL

It is difficult to imagine Council Hall in its original location at the southwest corner of the intersection of South Temple and Main Street, largely because it fits so nicely on its current site immediately to the south of the Utah State Capitol. Dedicated in 1866, Council Hall was one of the earliest public buildings in Utah. Plenty of local history was made here: meetings of the territorial legislature, the organization of the ZCMI, the board of health, and for a short period of time, temple endowments. This two-story building included offices, a large courtroom, and an immense council chamber, called the "Rose Room."

Plans to move Council Hall to its current location began in 1948, but it wasn't until 1961 that the building was dismantled stone by stone. The pioneers built the original structure for $70,000, but the cost of the reconstruction was $300,000. In its historic location, Council Hall sat diagonal from the Bishop's Storehouse, the central distribution point for the Mormon system of tithing, cooperative, and support during the 19th century. Both secular and religious activities transpired within, illustrating the tight connection between church and state in Utah Territory and symbolizing the unique blend of political, spiritual, and compassionate activities during the 19th century in Salt Lake City.

For 29 years, Council Hall was the seat of local government. These years were marked by the incredible colonization and expansion of the State of Deseret, confrontations with the U.S. government, the coming of the railroad, and the diversification of Utah's economy. Today, the Utah Travel Council operates an informational center out of the building. The Zion Natural History Association Bookstore is also located in Council Hall.

19th WARD MEETINGHOUSE/ SALT LAKE ACTING COMPANY

By 1890, Mormon Utah had survived the government's crusade to end polygamy, federal efforts to destroy the financial and theological power of the church, and territorial hegemony. With the advent of the railroad, outside influences also changed the local architecture. The next generation of churches looked more like buildings found in Europe than what one would expect in this western town. The 19th Ward Meetinghouse at 168 West 500 North, designed by Robert Bowman, deviates architecturally from the earlier generation of simple rectangular box meetinghouses. Meanwhile, the women of the ward had their own building next door, the Relief Society Hall. Built in 1908, the hall wasn't used for religious services, but rather for philanthropic activities.

The Salt Lake Acting Company debuted their first show in the 19th Ward Chapel in 1982. They've been around much longer, however—their annual production of *Saturday's Voyeur* has been a community tradition since the 1970s.

Built in 1890, Bowman used a combination of Asian, Byzantine, and even German renaissance influences on the meetinghouse. Its onion-shape dome, pinnacles, and elliptically vaulted ceiling distinguish it from other churches built during the era. The meetinghouse is shown here circa 1930.

Today the building is home to the Salt Lake Acting Company.

MARMALADE HILL

If there is anything to the real estate maxim, "Location, location, location," the Marmalade Hill district has it made. Situated to the west of the State Capitol building and north of the city, the neighborhood was originally built for working-class families. The rich diversity of its charming vernacular and Victorian buildings contrasts significantly with the larger, more high-class buildings immediately to the east. The architectural diversity of the neighborhood may be due to the fact that its early residents were primarily designers, builders, and artisans.

John Platts, a fruit grower, built one of the early homes in the area in 1856. While some houses are Victorian "painted ladies," other homes are in a Gothic style, where the detailing is expressed entirely in wood rather than the customary stone. The tradition of diversity in Marmalade Hill continues to this day, providing wonderful examples of early architecture in a modern setting, close to the heart of downtown.

Above left: This photo from 1909 shows the Salt Lake Temple and the Marmalade Hill district beyond. *Above right:* A brightly painted Victorian home is shown in 2009. This is a neighborhood that celebrates historic preservation with gusto, which plays out in the expression of personality, color, and delight.

At this time of this photo in 1905, West High was primarily a technical school.

West High is shown here in 2009. Its distinguished alums include LDS Church President Thomas S. Monson and Larry H. Miller, owner of the Utah Jazz.

The Technical High School, which was located just south of the main building, reflected the community's dedication to preparing students for work in the skilled trades. In this photo from 1915, students attend a blacksmith shop class.

WEST HIGH SCHOOL

Known during the 19th century as Union Square, the site of what is now West High School at 241 South 300 West was once a popular camping ground for immigrants who had just arrived in the valley. When the city was divided into blocks for settlement, the area was designated for educational use. During the 1880s and '90s, the block was home to a parade of educational facilities: the University of Deseret (later the University of Utah); the State School for the Deaf, Dumb and Blind; the Union Public grade school, and finally the Salt Lake High School. Today the school is known as West High.

The distinctive art deco style of the historic central section of West High features contrasting dark brick and white decorative trim. Two sculpture friezes jut out from the upper wall surface, made by well-known artist Mahonri Young, grandson of Brigham Young.

ALFRED W. McCUNE MANSION

More reminiscent of the shingle-style mansions of Newport, Rhode Island, the Alfred W. McCune Mansion, with its varied textures and dramatic colors, contrasts with the staid formality of the State Capitol building a block to the north. Spectacularly situated high above the street on the side of a hill, this 3-story, 21-room house includes a carriage house to the rear.

Alfred McCune was a railroad and mining magnate who in 1888 bought controlling interest in The Consolidated Railway and Power Company. After the McCunes moved to Los Angeles in 1920, they donated their home to the Latter-day Saints. The church began the McCune School of Art and Music in the building, which was located there until the Brigham Young University Salt Lake Center moved into the space in 1958. Since the 1970s, the McCune Mansion has been used as office and reception space.

Rare in Utah but popular in New England at the turn of the 19th and 20th centuries, the shingle style of architecture uses a variety of materials that range from red to dark brown in color: red sandstone, dark red brick, and red-brown roof tiles. The interior is as lush and sensuous as the exterior: Excellent design in woodwork, stonework, wall coverings, stained glass, and ceiling murals are present throughout. Another highlight is a mirrored ballroom on the upper level that was used by the McCunes for parties and dances; later generations used the room for large-scale meetings, parties, and wedding receptions.

Top: In this 1913 photo, the McCune Mansion was still a residence. *Bottom:* A tiered staircase leads to the mansion, as seen today. The McCune Mansion was listed on the National Register of Historic Places in 1974.

INDEX